Desperate Farmwives

Check out the blog *Desperate Farmwives*
www.desperatefarmwives.weebly.com

Desperate Farmwives

Elisha Wells Stroupe

An imprint of HoCo Media, L.L.C.
hocomomedia.com

Cover photography by Brittany Minor Photography

ISBN-13: 9780692041925

For John, the best first husband a girl could ask for

CONTENTS

Desperate
Farmwives

INTRODUCTION

A few years ago, it occurred to me that some of my acquaintances thought I was out of place on a farm, basically because they flat out said that they could never have imagined me on a farm. They thought I wouldn't stay around my hometown, and the farm was the last place they thought I would end up. When I say "they," I mean a former teacher, one friend, and the lady at the gas station, but all-in-all, it felt like a smack in the face, as if I had let them down. I had been groomed and was destined to rule the world, but instead, I have chosen to rule the roost. Technically, they probably just hoped I'd at least live somewhere with a Super Target, not really rule the world, but the dreams of a rural dweller can sometimes be simple, yet, oh so fantastic.

After more than ten years on this farm, I've decided that this is exactly where I should be (as long as I get a hotel stay elsewhere every once in a while because no one loves to steal hotel soap more than I do). I've just needed to incorporate more of myself into the farm, as the farm has already done its damage to me. I'm seriously slipping. I didn't even argue recently when my husband put a calf in the hatchback of my car, and then the calf pooped back there. It made that high-pitched crying calf sound that's more like Maaaaa than Moooo right before it pooped, so maybe it wasn't sick. Maybe it was constipated, or so my husband says as an excuse on how my sacrifice may have saved that cow. It clearly could have just pooped in the field, but I didn't complain. It seemed completely normal, well, until I was left cleaning it up. Yes, the farm has done a fair amount of damage to me (and my car).

This book is a collection of stories that I've put together, my therapy of things that once irritated me, but with a little time, I've managed to twist into humorous little tidbits about our unorthodox farm life. It's also just another project I've come up with to avoid helping with farm chores, so...there's that too.

Yes, I'm talking about you, little calf.

A Desperate Farm Wife

IF YOU CAN'T BEAT 'EM, JOIN 'EM

When I first moved to the farm in 2005, my now husband and I lived in a trailer on his parents' dairy farm. We had regular jobs with regular hours. We didn't have a lot, but it was nice. Everything was organized; I was working on a garden in spite of the herd of my father-in-law's cows trying to get at it, and our home and yard usually looked nice when the hot wire kept the cow patties at bay. We went out on the weekends, every weekend, all weekend. We had a life. But sadly, we had dreams.

Dreams are an equal combination of soul-sucking heartache and soul-building euphoria, but my husband and I had the dreams before we had kids so we had enough sleep at the time to chase the euphoria. He wanted to solely work on the farm, I wanted to be a writer, and we both wanted to build a house to start a family. First, I started teaching so I'd have summers off to write. If teaching doesn't drain your social life and creativity, I don't know what does. Believe me, I have many short stories and uncompleted novels from those summers that I could torture you with. Then my husband and I got married and that also does its damage. We saved all our money and started the house. We were so naive. Lastly, I got knocked up and he quit his job to be the full-time cattleman/dad.

Currently, we live in a construction zone, but it's fitting as all our other dreams seem somewhat half complete as well, which I've learned is normal for ambitious people. We have an unnatural capacity to tack things on to our original dream and then beat ourselves up for not completing a list that never ends. As far as the house goes, it's as if we have one foot in normalcy and one out. The first winter we had no insulation, and it was so cold that I threw a hissy fit and screamed, "I can't live like this!" Magically, insulation appeared when I came home from work the next day. I should have been embarrassed by my behavior, but I got a glimpse of the life of a spoiled kid. Valuable lesson learned: hissy fit - 1 / unsuspecting husband - 0.

Some parts of our home look 100% normal. We have the most beautiful brick retaining wall next to a poorly mowed yard with ruts the size of tractor tires because we sporadically have to pull large trucks onto the yard for continual projects. People pull up to the house, praising how wonderful it looks, until they peek in the front door and find a construction zone with plywood, insulation, and 2x4s, minus the work crew. Last, but not least, there is not a picket fence around our yard, but a hot wire that is never hot when animals are actually in the vicinity.

This hot wire situation leads to the fact that the farm really has done its damage on me. My husband jokes about mowing the lawn, asking why he needs to when there are perfectly good animals to do it for him. "I'll just let the sheep in," he says with a playful laugh. I can never understand why he laughs like he's joking because he just does it anyway. It's not a joke – it's reality. He very rarely mows the grass, and when he does, it's with a bent-blade lawn mower, so honestly, the sheep would probably do a better job. My husband gets out the mower with no game plan whatsoever. The grass ends up uneven, in large clumps, with big spots that he misses and just pretends that he never even saw.

So as I sat staring out the window at the uneven grass on a fall afternoon, thinking about the careers in which I would have been a beast - neurosurgeon, VP of Advertising in Don Draper's office, political speech writer for a politician who's in big trouble - it takes me a moment to notice the invaders. As I snap out of my New York City dream career, I see one white lamb tentatively take a step over the hot wire, then a tan ewe follows, then a whole herd makes the natural decision to follow, and I just sit quietly. I could go out there and chase them back, but that would be wasteful. They are already in the yard. I might as well let them fertilize it, eat the clumps, and get rid of all the uneven spots left behind by the old, hold-the-key-just-right mower. I'll just sit here and not make a move so they don't see me through the windows. Oh well, if you can't beat 'em, join 'em. I couldn't have gotten that story in New York City, if not for the sheep, definitely for the code violations.

* * *

And so, my therapeutic journey was born that October as I watched sheep invade my yard. I then started writing my farm tales, to put a humorous spin on all the things that made me want to drop to the ground in our yard, arch my back like a toddler, kick and scream, pull my hair out and claw my face, wondering if I should have tried a little harder in college rather than spend a lot of brain cells on what we wittily called Senior Seminar, a.k.a. cheap drinks at the local bars. I've done the tantrum thing recently, and it didn't work. It only got my favorite sweatpants muddy and a roll of the eyes from my husband.

His name is John, by the way. One of his biggest complaints is that I never introduce him, so I thought, "Why change now? Might as well introduce him after a whole page of making fun of him." Hopefully, you're still reading. John sold those particular sheep not long after I wrote the insightful introduction to our crazy life when I started my blog *Desperate Farmwives*, giving me a few options for the last mow of the season to deal with the lawn.

1. Mow it myself. HAHAHAHAHA!
2. Let the cows in to do it and risk dodging large cow patties as I hop from place to place.
3. Find the remaining sheep that dodged getting shipped off. I don't think there was a leftover sheep, but John thought there was one, and this was his sly way of getting me to search the farm for it.
4. Just wait for winter and let the snow and ice cover it.

As usual, I decided to write about our yard, take pictures, post them on my blog, and wait for the magic to happen. It's not pretty, but John will mow pretty regularly if he thinks the world wide web is going to judge him. And that, dear reader, is what drives me to continue writing. To shame others, of course. Oh yeah, and ambition, I forgot about that pesky thing called ambition.

Life Quote: Ambition's a bitch. ~ John Stroupe, my highly philosophical husband.

John, A Very Indulgent Husband

since he's read and approved all the slanderous things I've written about him

∞

Before I get into describing the chaos around me, or what I deem to be chaos and everyone else around here thinks perfectly normal, I should introduce you to my husband John. He's the one who brought me into this fold of money-saving, widely read, quirky farm people. He is 90% a product of his family and 10% a product of sarcasm and inappropriateness, but the older he gets, the louder the 10% becomes. He's a gem and a turd at the same time. But I love him, more than I want him to know, so please don't ruin this judgmental facade I have going with him. It really gets things done around the house and farm.

∞

THE MAN BEHIND THE MADNESS

John does everything the hard way, something he learned from his father. The hard way is the cheaper way, as he sees it, but he thinks he's better at weighing the difference between money saved and time spent on some of his projects around here. I'm not 100% sure he's correct in that estimate. He spent high school sneaking Louis L'Amour novels in his math textbook to look like he was absorbing the fascinating workings of algebra, so he's never been great at math. I think the lack of math skills is one reason he is so tight with money. He just wants to make sure there's plenty there. Or, it's just generation upon generation of nurturing this thriftiness that has made him this way.

He comes from Norwegians who came to the U.S. to escape hard economic times and thought their paradise would be in Wisconsin, and since it became the cheese state, they were surprisingly correct, except for that pesky thing called snow, and since they were some thick-skinned people, they enjoyed it. They were dairy farmers who didn't have time to spend money and then they lived through the Depression and didn't have any money to spend. His family then moved to Missouri and found the tropical weather to be much better for them, and they could just road trip to Wisconsin every now and then to get a car load of cheese. Yes, they do this. Recently, we also reached the age one needs to be to drive to Wisconsin for a car load of cheese. It seems to be the age of thirty-seven.

I am thankful for the generations of frugality because small dairy farms are not a profitable venture anymore, so my father-in-law did his own thing. He spent years as the delivery man of his raw milk dairy when selling to a company no longer proved profitable for a small farm. When he retired, my husband bought part of the farm for livestock. Please don't ask me what crops we grow. It's only livestock. This isn't Texas, so we don't own a ranch; we own a farm. I get that question a lot. We do grow thorn trees like nobody's business though. Maybe I can find some medicinal purpose for that...Hmmm….

My husband likes to use what he's got around him to create what success he can, so he might like this idea. He is a tightwad, but he was made that way. Although, he will spend money on beer, Snickers, and a hotel if vacationing (the cheapest hotel) because camping is not his style.

I've repeated the phrase, "You have to spend money to make money," multiple times when he's asked me about a purchase he wants to make, from trucks, to tractors, to brush hogs, and dozers, but when I say it, his eye starts to twitch and he clutches his wallet like he's in a sketchy alley in New York City. Then he comes home with a $500 truck that needs numerous repairs but will basically get the job done (for a couple of years, so that's a good investment).

Don't think he needs my permission to buy any of these things. He only asks because anything over $20 is a large purchase for him and he needs to do the research. He will ask my opinion even though he already knows my answer, which is always to buy something that will last and spend a little extra money, and then he'll do the opposite. That's why he has money (even though I've never seen it), and I don't. I'm not the only source he comes to though. He also asks a friend, his dad, his grandpa, other farmers from all over the country whom he knows only through text messages and an online forum called *AgTalk*. He's a mess, but a mess with jars of money buried in the yard (or that's what I've been trying to dig up for the last few years). I'm starting to think he's led me to believe it so I'll eventually dig enough for a new pond.

He's also Mr. Antisocial until he's in a crowd of people. I have to trick, bribe, or threaten him into attending an event, party, or to take me on a date. Then, within five minutes of being in a crowd of people he says or does something wildly inappropriate and becomes the life of the party. It's his super power. It's also really irritating to me. When we are in the car, on our way to any crowd, whether family, friends, colleagues, or strangers, I give him the speech that coincides with the group we will be meeting.

"Don't say this, don't say that, don't tell that particular joke because you'll offend this person, don't say this because so-and-so will freak out, blah, blah, blah."

And what does he do as soon as we arrive? Exactly what I told him not to, and people love him for it. When he first met my roommates from college, I spent the six-hour drive to Sioux City, Iowa, location of Briar Cliff University, my alma mater, quizzing him on what not to say and within minutes of being there he combined every offensive thing I said not to say into one vulgar joke. And they laughed hysterically. Again, it's really irritating.

The following is a list of important events in our life that should have been red flags:

1. He described our first date as an adventure, taking me to a cave, a farm with historic significance, and then making dinner for me. Add it all up and he spent $0, unless you

include gas money and how much dinner would have cost had he shopped for it. By the way, the meat and bread came from his parents. I think he may have purchased the potatoes. Ladies, if a man suggests a date like this, you will either spend the rest of your life frugally or you will be dead because he only intended to kill you in the cave and didn't want to feed you an expensive dinner beforehand because what would be the point?

2. He asked me to move in with him as I was making him dinner. That's what motivated him to take the next important step in our relationship - food. But honestly, it was on fried round steak and mashed potatoes and gravy night, so who can blame him?
3. When he shook me awake from a glorious pre-children afternoon nap, I rolled over to find an engagement ring in my face. "Will you?" he asked. Until I had children, I was one of those annoying people who is super chipper when woken up, which he was generally annoyed with, but I think he used it to his advantage on this one - pick the time of day when I'm the happiest and hope for the best.
4. When I was pregnant with both of our boys, he compared me to a cow, my pregnancy to a cow's gestation, and all my breastfeeding dilemmas to what he knew about dairy cows, which is a lot.

As you have probably noticed, I had to skip our wedding because he was pretty awesome for that, and then he took me to Ireland on our honeymoon, so that takes away from the whole tightwad motif I'm trying to create. Please strike that from the record, and disregard those comments.

There are many other things that irritate me about him. He reads faster than I do, so he'll pick up what I'm reading, finish it, then proceed to give me the juicy details that I'd like to read on my own. He never hears a baby crying even when it's his turn, even when I take his covers and kick him a few times. He can never be serious, and he keeps joking even when I start screaming, "Where are the f*&#%!@ Twix bars?!" Ugh! It's rough around here.

Thankfully, I love him. Just like Einstein's first and second wives, Michael Jackson and Lisa Marie Presley, and George and Laura Bush, I'll stand by my quirky guy. Let's just hope he doesn't feel the need to start writing stories about me. So far, I'm coming up roses, so let's just let the reader think I'm the long-suffering wife for now.

Life Quote: I hate people. ~ John, at least once a day.

Ham and Beans

FARMER FACEBOOK

As I've mentioned, John spends a lot of time reading. We live in a house filled with books. John's dinner conversation is usually some weird fact from *Uncle John's Bathroom Reader* or a 1950's article from the *National Geographic.* That's a wide range of literary style there. Our home construction plans are thwarted daily by new plans of where we're going to put another shelf for our books because we are slowly growing our own library. John's a very fast reader and he reads an enormous amount of material about farming and ranching, a lot of weather-related articles, some books, and an occasional *Maxim.* Before I moved in with him, he didn't have a computer for reading material, and after I moved in, he slowly started realizing its benefits.

First, he just wanted to see the weather. You could say it was for the benefit of his cows, but it was back in the day when we both had employers, so it was mostly to see when we'd get a snow day. Someone should do a study on construction worker/educator marriage combos and birth rates nine months after a snow day. I bet the findings are, well, obvious.

Once he mastered the weather, he needed email for a few documents from farmers and the local USDA office. After asking me to look up things for him on the world wide web a few times, he realized that all the information he could ever want was at his fingertips and it really wasn't that hard to find. So, he started to hunt and peck his way to a PhD in cattle, sheep, pigs, and Craigslist. He found a brush hog and hay for sale.

Completely amazed, he said, "This thing has stuff from everywhere, then you find exactly what you need for sale ten miles away from someone you know. I just found a $300 Festiva just down the road."

I didn't realize I was creating a monster.

Now he is a well-read internet connoisseur. He even found what I call "Farmer Facebook." It's actually called *AgTalk* and it's a forum with lots of different subject areas such as machinery, crops, livestock, and a section called "Kitchen Table" where they discuss anything from recipes, personal businesses, and weight loss. From what he's shown me, you can find an inappropriate joke on any page, so it's a site built just for him.

He's learned how to save a bottle calf that's gotten cold and doesn't have any strength - put a little coffee in their bottle and that perks them right up. How we didn't know this beforehand, I'll never know. We've always known coffee saves lives, but I guess we were only thinking in human terms. It's worked two out of three times, so for a bottle calf, we're considering that a win. He's also learned the meaning to lyrics from the old Kentucky Headhunters song "Dumas Walker." The song says, "We'll get a slaw burger, fries, and a bottle of Ski," and he recently learned from Farmer Facebook that Ski is a soda made in Tennessee. I really appreciated this find because it's a great song of which I don't know all the words to but loudly mumble through parts like that. He has also made friends with a couple of other farmers who have offered us a place to crash if we ever want to take a vacation to Texas or Florida. I've tried to explain that the internet is not a good place to make friends who automatically ask you to stay in their homes, but I guess he hasn't seen the number of serial killers targeting their online acquaintances who end up on the news. Ironically, they are usually from Florida or Texas.

He says the forum stays pretty civil even throughout the inappropriate jokes, until late winter, and then everyone starts fighting. Bringing up politics, religion, cattle prices, or vegans can cause quite a stir around mid-February when they all need a little vitamin D, sunshine, and more hay.

Life Quote: If you have chcken litter spread I would be careful of when it was done, like not the week your landlord is having a fancy wedding reception. The neighbor just to the north of me had some spread a few years ago everybody was asking me if I had cows dying. It takes a good rain to make the smell go away. Combo of B.O, Feet and Farts. Sure did make the grass grow though!! ~ John, from Farmer Facebook with no grammatical corrections. This is seriously how he presents himself online.

CATTLE CONFERENCE - THAT'S A REAL THING

Farmer Facebook even supplied my lifelong learning husband with his cattle philosophical hero: Bud Williams. He was a cattleman who produced numerous videos about correct stockmanship to save a producer money by keeping their cows stress free, which in turn keeps them healthy, especially calves who are immune to nothing. In my opinion, this philosophy is just that elusive quality that neither my husband nor I possess - patience - but John says it's much more than that. He just doesn't want to admit it because he hasn't quite conquered it yet.

After joining the email newsletter of this patience program, my husband discovered the Bud Summit. I was continually going to teaching conferences where I'd come home with stories of letting loose with a bunch of librarians and teachers, and he wanted to get in on the conference action. If you haven't gone to a conference in your field, I highly recommend it, especially if it's an overnight conference. At the most, you'll learn a lot about what you love to do (if you love to do it), and at the very least, you'll have a day away to readjust to a brighter perspective of your chosen profession. Your profession is like your children – it can be really annoying, but after a 24-hour break, it doesn't seem quite that bad.

John invited me along to his cattle conference once, just the two of us. It was the date weekend I'd never asked for. I really, really tried to pay attention to the market research, but I'm not good with charts and graphs and legitimate ways to make money, so I quickly spaced out and started working on this writing gig, writing a funny story about my husband while trying to hide it from him as he sat right next to me. After the lunch break, I didn't even go back and did what I usually do when I'm in a hotel room with a ridiculous number of television channels - I watched a *Real Housewives of New Jersey* marathon. Those ladies could have used a few patience lessons from Bud Williams, but he probably would have had a hard time herding them, except to the bar.

Since I was pretty useless as a conference buddy, I decided to make the following years a mini vacation for my sons. We always had lots of fun checking out the local attractions in a new city, but one trip was not memorable for the zoo, the parks, or the massive amounts of junk food. We will remember this trip for the insanely awful hotel that these cattle people chose to stay in.

We had stayed in this hotel before for the previous conferences. It always seemed a little sketchy, but we skated by without any mishaps. It was super cheap too, so it's hard to pass that up as long as you come out alive in the end. As long as it had a pool and a free breakfast, I could make it work.

We were in the better of the two hotels of this chain in the particular town we were in. I don't want to get sued so I'm not naming the town or the hotel name. You're on your own so use the clues hidden in this story. I can't have all the fun, can I? When we first went to the hotel, I attempted to get there without Google Maps and these two hotels of the same chain are on opposite ends of town on the same street. The one we stayed in was in between the regular chains like Hampton Inn and Holiday Inn. The one I accidentally went to was between a firework stand and a liquor store. It also had a gentlemen's club attached to the hotel. My husband was very disappointed when I realized my mistake and quickly headed for the correct hotel. Besides that one mishap, we didn't have any complaints, but chaos was going to happen, and it happened on our fourth year at the conference. That particular year we weren't so lucky.

First, when we arrived, we received an outside door room, which I assume is unsafe since alleged rapers and robbers don't have to walk past the 120-pound, nerdy guy at the front desk during the night shift. Oh well, after driving three hours with a three-year-old, I was willing to take any room so my son Aiden could burn some steam flying from one double bed to another, to the recliner, and back again. Then we got into the room, and it was a smoking room. Ugh! This didn't fly with me. I was pregnant, eight months pregnant, which I had spent in a constant state of nausea, so the smell just made me feel even worse, but the hotel was booked solid and we couldn't get into another room until late that evening, if they could even find a nonsmoking room at all, so we had to deal with it. So much for making a very detailed reservation, huh.

Strike one nerdy guy at the front desk…

After we dropped off our bags, we went to the gas station before the meetings started so my husband could get beer. The conference is really just a ruse. It's really the one weekend out of the year when unsociable people become sociable because of their love of cows and beer. I get it though because I was once a librarian. Replace cows with books and it's like the same conference. Upon our return to the room, I scanned the key card quickly, slowly, wiggled it around, and it just wouldn't work on our door, a sign of trouble to come, but hindsight is 20/20. My husband quickly ran up to the front desk and got it fixed, and we went on our way. He went to the conference holding his six-pack like a brief case, and my son and I went hiking at a nearby nature trail.

When we returned, we went swimming. This lasted about 20 minutes, five of which were actually spent swimming since we had to make multiple trips back to the room because my son would climb out yelling, "I have to poop! I have to poop!"

Back at the room, I dried Aiden off and turned on a cartoon so I could go to the bathroom and wiggle my pregnant body out of my swimsuit, which was a workout. I pulled two muscles, and for a moment, thought I was going into labor. Just as I got changed, I heard the door open. Thinking my husband was returning, I continued brushing my teeth at the sink until I saw the door shut through the reflection in the mirror and no one had entered. I walked toward the door wondering if I had put the chain on and thinking my husband must not be able to enter, when my three-year-old said, "That lady was looking at me."

Strike two sketchy hotel camouflaging itself in franchise-hotel row...

"What lady?" I asked.

"The lady that opened the door."

"That wasn't your daddy?" I asked frantically as I finally reached for the door to check it out. No one was outside.

I continued to ask my three-year-old who it was that opened the door, but I was distracting him from his cartoons. After examining the door, I convinced myself that I hadn't shut it completely. It was a little tricky, and someone must have just come to the wrong room and opened the door because it hadn't been latched for the key card to work. It was disarming, I was panicking, yet my three-year-old could only tell me, "That lady was looking at me," as he pushed me from his line of sight of the television.

Was this going to be some repressed memory that would eventually make him shy around women later in life? Would he be forever scarred by this encounter? We'd all whisper about his strange behavior stemming from "the lady who was looking at him." It sounds creepy, right? Not really? All that was seriously running through my head. Looking back now, I wish it would have scarred him a little. He does not know stranger danger and likes to ask people inappropriate questions. He needs something to hold him back.

In the back of my head the latch idea didn't seem legit, but I had convinced myself. When my husband returned, I just happened to have the door open, checking the latch again. I told him about it, and he made sure to chain the door when he came in and double checked to make sure it was latching. We went to bed. Of course, he went easily and I was paranoid, waking at every noise.

Finally, sleep came after doing the pregnant lady rotation about thirty times, trying to get the baby in my belly to stop laying on my bladder, but sleep quickly went. At 2:00 A.M., woken by a slight breeze like any mom, I heard a rattling at the door, and my super sensitive mom ears perked up quickly, assisted by restless pregnant woman mode, but the rest of my senses trailed behind.

"Oh my God, they're coming back to kidnap my three-year-old," I thought to myself as I groggily tried to jump out of bed. At eight months pregnant, I was like a turtle on its back trying to rock myself into a position in which I'd be able to lift myself out of bed. I wanted to kick myself for allowing my son to sleep in the bed closest to the door since my body was not catching up to my brain. Then the door actually opened (thank goodness for the chain), and my heart jumped into my throat. In what sounded like a low drunken dinosaur's voice spewing from my drool covered lips, I screamed, "GET OUT! Get out of here!"

A clearly frightened woman on the other side quickly shut the door saying, "Oh, I'm so sorry, sorry!"

She had no idea there was a drunken dinosaur in the room.

By the time I got to the door and looked out the window, no

one was there. My husband was completely startled, sleeping through most of it even though I was wailing my arms at him in that sissy girl way you see women do in the movies. My son didn't even budge. He was happily sleeping away looking like an angel. I explained what happened to my husband and called the front desk, but of course, no one answered.

Strike three...and end of game...Mommy's mad!

So, it was time. They had pushed me to the limit. They had asked for it. I was going to march my pregnant-self up to the front desk and give them a piece of my mind (if I could make it inside the hotel without getting killed). I was still slightly concerned, as I booked it to the lobby, that the frightened lady behind the door was really a kidnapper, but my dinosaur voice had scared her away. She might have been watching me at that very moment and realized it was just a congested pregnant chick whom she could easily take.

When I entered the lobby undisturbed, the 120-pound nerdy desk clerk knew what was coming. He looked like he was steeling himself for a smack in the face. It was obvious he already knew something because he was apologizing all over the place when he saw my mommy battle face charging – well, waddle stomping - to his desk.

I ranted for a while with my list of problems which is summarized below:

- outside door
- smoking room
- key card not working
- someone entering earlier (I then realized I had latched the door)
- someone entering in the middle of the night
- waking up a pregnant woman and trying to give her a heart attack
- my son could have been kidnapped

- complimentary breakfast better have sausage links or I will burn this mother down
- not answering the phone when I called
- a manager better call me the next day so I can chew multiple people out

Once my rant ended, he explained that something was wrong with their computer, and it wasn't saving the information that someone had already occupied that room, so they were basically giving away our room when someone would check-in. Each time that would happen, our key card would deactivate, therefore, someone had been in our room when we went to the gas station too. So far, they had given away our room three times and still hadn't fixed it. This was not a large hotel with hundreds of rooms and the same guy had been at the front desk since we checked in. He didn't realize he had given our room away three times!

I didn't trust his memory or his computer and told him to put a Post-it on it that said our room was occupied. I would have left right at that moment if I was just with my husband, but moving a toddler in the middle of the night would have been a nightmare. After emphasizing again that a manager BETTER call me in the morning, I returned to my room in a huff. I double-checked the door latch, chained it, put a chair in front of it, and lay in bed with my son, blocking him from the would-be kidnappers. I was sure they were coming. And no, I did not sleep.

The next morning, we ate our complimentary breakfast, with sausage links I might add, and my husband went to the conference. My son and I got ready for another full day of fun out on the town. He was excited, and I was exhausted, but my motto is fake it 'til you make it. Vacation should be so jammed-packed with activity and fun that everyone is happy to head home. My husband believes I am the vacation soul crusher. I'm just the activities director that you never asked for. On this particular trip though, less than 24 hours in and I was ready to head home.

As I packed up our stuff sleepily, tempted to just take a really short five-hour nap, what do you know, the housekeepers tried to get in because the room was still listed as vacant in the computer. I ranted and raved to them, two ladies who probably thought I was insane, but since I was pregnant, they took pity on me and called the front desk to see what was going on. The bright yellow Post-it had been discarded when the new shift arrived. By this time, I was giving up, but they gave them the what-for that I was too tired to give. They were horrified for me and took up the good fight.

Eventually (two weeks later), a very nice manager did get back with me and our room was free. Very nice, but very late. My husband saw the free room as an extra bonus during a very educational and all-around enjoyable weekend. His only regret was that this didn't happen on a regular fun family holiday because that hotel room would have been tax deductible for the cattle conference anyway. He's always thinking! Obviously, he felt safe that any criminals would have gotten me first, since I was closer to the door. I saw it as my right since cattlemen have terrible taste in hotels. There's a Drury Inn next door, so if I go again, you'll know where to find me. At the free hors d'oeuvre and cocktail event they have every evening, and the kids will be at grandma's house.

Life Quote: Remember when that lady saw me naked. ~ My son after the incident. Oh, did I not mention that he was just chilling out with no Spiderman underwear?

Airing of Grievances

∞

This book is not to complain about my life on the farm, although it will certainly look like it as you read further. It's just my way of discussing the things in life that I'm not yet accustomed to, and in turn, I become accustomed to them by making them funny. At the time, were they funny? No, absolutely not. Life on this farm can be irritating, aggravating, backward, and downright disastrous, but it's fun most of the time. So please don't think I'm complaining. I just can't let some of these stories go without sharing them with the world. Where else are you going to learn about farm animals, heathen children, and passive-aggressive behavior? A rural high school, you say. You are correct, but you'll learn about it here too.

∞

SACRIFICES

My biggest hang-up about farm life is winter. I should clarify that statement – my biggest hang-up about *life* is winter. I'm not a winter person. Global warming is happening people (and a little part of me is okay if winter were gone for a few years before the planet implodes on itself). Anything about winter on a farm just sucks; there's really no other word to describe it. Do not believe those postcards and movies where the farm family is sitting inside enjoying their hot chocolate while Dad comes in from the snow with adorable, slightly rosy cheeks to a smiling family. That does not happen. Everybody's cold and cranky from the lack of sun. When Dad comes in, the toddlers are screaming, begging to go outside because they have already destroyed every room in the house, and the wife is crying because it's already dark and she wanted to get out of the house for a walk.

"Oh, you say it's -2° outside. I need a break from these monster children!" she yells through clenched teeth.

Well, that's how we roll in this house anyway.

On one of those last warm days before winter sets in, I usually spend some time prepping my car, making sure it's good and ready for the winter ahead, and a winter on this farm is especially rough on cars since the two-car garage is full of farm equipment and/or junk. I get the back-up ice scraper, de-icer, extra gloves, a blanket, and some snacks together. In case I ever get stuck during the winter, I need the peace of mind that I won't be "hangry" too. The only place that I've been stuck during winter weather is actually in our driveway, but five minutes of being stuck could be used wisely eating breakfast #2 or the afternoon snack/meal. It could save my husband's life if I eat a snack before he comes to help me out of my predicament. When I do this prep work, I am always nostalgic for my old car.

No amount of winterizing could prepare that Mustang for winter, but I sure looked cool driving it, even if I could only drive it five miles an hour because of winter weather from November to March. It was not made for winter, just like me, and definitely not farm life, but we were a team and held out for seven years.

I know that a Mustang is a terrible choice for a farm vehicle, but I must remind you that I purchased it before I met my husband, to be specific, three months before I met him. I had no intention of putting her through this. We had big plans to live in a city. I'd write novels, and she'd wait around until I needed a break, and we'd cruise to clear my head. The Mustang gene was in my blood. My family had an obsession with Mustangs, but I was the only one who hadn't invested in a garage and a back-up vehicle for bad weather.

I got my first Mustang when I was 16. It was a 5.0, black with silver racing stripes. It was very, very fast. My suggestion to parents: Never, ever let your teenager drive a sports car, no matter how much you trust them, absolutely never. I was the good kid and my mom still gave me a million rules: Wear your seatbelt, don't leave town, only one person in the car with you, drive the speed limit. Of course, I broke every single one of those, all on the first day of getting my license. I did not have my seatbelt on when I drove two hours to St.

Louis the morning after I got my license. Well, at least there was only one other person in the car. Why did we drive to St. Louis? No reason at all other than to break the rules because my friend and I immediately drove back after, driving through downtown and then making it a competition if I could get better time on the way back.

A 16-year-old is not going to say, "Why, yes, of course, I will only use a quarter of this speedometer."

A 16-year-old is going to say, "I wonder if the speedometer will get stuck if I get it to the max."

Before graduating college, I bought a brand new Mustang, which is the last brand new car I will ever buy because age has taught me that that's an absolute waste of money, but it was a sign (to myself) that I was going places. It turned out to be a good example of irony because just a few months later I started dating my husband and the Mustang was relegated to the outdoors, in a semi-grassy, semi-gravel spot. That was not the place I pictured I would be going.

> *Side Note Soapbox*: Make your kids purchase, repair, and insure their own cars. They will learn about responsibility, and have awesome credit ratings and insurance rates at a very young age. Also, it will save you insurance hikes when your eldest rear ends three people in the matter of months in your Geo Prizm and ruins the sweet you-can-be-on-my-insurance deal for their more responsible, younger sister. Thanks a lot, Big Bro! I'm not bitter at all.

Okay, back to the point of this story, to complain about my husband's backward ways, not about my brother's absolutely terrible, losing-all-his-points-on-his-license, awful driving skills.

The farm really did a number on my Mustang. The car was pretty, but not convenient of course, although many of the problems would never have occurred on another farm, just on my husband's farm. Like any other Mustang, rocks, mud, ice, and snow can be a problem. If you own a Mustang in a not-so-friendly sports car area, you have to learn these techniques since it's rear wheel drive:

- Rocking it back and forth
- Pushing
- Driving it in reverse until you hit a highway
- Slamming the gas to spinning tires just out of anger, which doesn't work, but makes you feel a little better
- Kitty litter in bulk to throw under the tires during bad weather or some other technique that works on every other car but only makes a Mustang move an inch (hence, kitty litter in BULK)
- If you are completely alone, put a brick on the gas pedal and push yourself. If you've driven a Mustang in the snow, you know it's not going to take off without you. It will just move an inch from the slush, and the wheels will turn in place on top of the snow, giving you plenty of time to get back in and drive with one leg out the door, to walk it to the nearest clear road.

As you've probably guessed by now, I went through an inordinate amount of very expensive tires.

On one very difficult day, I was having a ton of trouble getting my car out of the driveway. It was not snowy, just a little icy. Usually this was not a problem because I could get traction on the gravel in our driveway, but on this particular morning, I'd go about two or three feet and get stuck. It was 6:00 A.M., and my husband miraculously didn't hear me cussing up a storm or revving the engine for the preceding 30 minutes. He was still asleep because he was on a road crew vacation (winter layoff).

I was on my own, in an utter agitation about being late for work (late for me is not being two hours early). Routine is essential for me, so yes, I was overreacting, but my students needed me on a routine for their personal sanity. I grabbed a flashlight to investigate what was slowing me down as ten or fifteen cows surrounded my car waiting for their punchline.

My front right tire had been stopped by a frozen cow patty.

That's right, every dang time my tires spun, it was from the ridiculous number of giant frozen cow patties in our driveway. I needed a good run at it so I could get going fast enough to overtake them. Before I got started, I revved my engine loud enough and screamed out the window to chase those condescending dairy cows away. I had to back up to a spot that had a good clean length, which was hard to find. It took a while and the cows kept creeping back up to taunt me. Then I finally got to the gate, opened it, and had to start all over again.

After wasting an hour and a quarter tank of gas, I finally got out. All that time, all that noise, 30 feet from our bedroom window, and not a peep from my husband. I called my husband as I left the gate standing wide open. Stopping was not an option at this point. Of course, I got his voicemail because he was still soundly sleeping. The very colorful message I left started with, "*@%^# cow patties" and ended with, "close the *#%@*(@ gate before the @%^# cows get out!"

My Mustang and I wouldn't let winter weather drag us down. For seven winters we fought the good fight, very carefully and very slowly. Even when I was pregnant, I was determined to keep my impractical sports car, hauling my very wide butt out of it every day. Everyone told me, "It's hard to get a car seat in there," but I didn't care about that. I could be a mommy and be cool. Then I had the baby. The cutest baby in the world, I might add. Well, one of the two cutest babies in the world because I have two children. It was not getting the pumpkin seat in and out that caused the problem. That would have been a plus because my muscle tone would have been better than Michelle Obama's.

The problem was finding a place to sit after the pumpkin seat took up all the space. It was oddly reminiscent of when I first bought the car and realized that my cooler would not fit in the trunk. It wasn't a huge cooler, just your run-of-the-mill Igloo cooler that can fit a lot of sandwiches, some sodas, and oh, I don't know, two cases of beer. Just an estimate from the mathematics learned by every college graduate of a private Catholic school. My high school and lifelong friend Teri and I decided to put the cooler in the backseat since it didn't fit in the trunk, but we were then forced to move our seats up really far to give it room.

Similarly, my son's seat was on the back-passenger side, so the driver was fine, but the passenger up front had to sit forehead to windshield.

"The road looks really close," my husband said squeamishly as he tried to squeeze into the seat.

The adjustable seat was adjusted forward instead of its real purpose – to lean back. We then started driving chauffeur-style because it was just too frightening when a bug would splat what seemed like millimeters from your face. My husband would drive and I would sit in the back with my son. When babies sleep almost all day, this was a very lonely seat, especially without control of the radio. I couldn't take the Brownfield Network Ag News for one more minute.

Finally, I caved and bought a mommy car and sold the Mustang to a nice older family who had grown children and could go back and collect some of their youth that had been stolen from them by demanding little beasts. So please, encourage your friends to buy this book, or buy it for them, so I can get an extremely long, heated driveway, and a Mustang to renew my pride. Think of it as an act of charity and write it off on your taxes. I'll even let you hang out in it for a while. Same goes for a summer house in Ireland and a cabin in the Black Hills. Let's make it happen, people!

Life Quote(s): That car is not safe, you need to make her get a safer car. ~ A farmer friend of my husband.

And: Well, you'll be divorced in six months. That's what happened to me when my ex-wife sold her sports car. ~ Same farmer friend after I sold the car.

HOW TO GET THINGS FIXED IN A PASSIVE-AGGRESSIVE MANNER

Sometimes things that need fixing around here go without for a very long time. It's another aggravation of mine that I'm learning to deal with by ignoring or using *YouTube* to attempt to fix it myself. If I can't find the right fix-it video, I head straight for a meditation video to help me ignore what I can't fix. It could be cost or time that prevents any action, but you can't take ten steps without running into one of these problems:

- giant potholes in which you could lose a car (such as a Festiva)
- a toilet bowl that runs if you don't hold the handle just right and cross your fingers as you do it
- a shower that clogs every time you're in it, hence the plunger relegated only to the shower
- a door hanging off the entertainment center
- a washer that always needs an extra spin cycle and a dryer that always needs two cycles to dry

- mud where there should be grass
- grass where there should be gravel
- gravel tracked into my house from muddy boots
- a refrigerator that pees

These are just some of the things that I notice on a daily basis and repeatedly remind myself to take care of, but I never get to it or the problem is only worsened by neglect. Obviously, I've left off anything from the farm because what I declare a problem, my husband thinks is perfectly fine, therefore, I have plenty of material about which to write.

After ten years with my husband, I've finally realized a method of getting things fixed around here in a rather sneaky way. It somewhat stems from my husband's theory of, "Do it wrong, and they'll never ask you again," but it didn't dawn on me until I saw my mother-in-law closing a gate. Magically, without saying a word (just mumbling some cuss words), she taught me a very valuable farm wife lesson.

After leaving her house one afternoon, I came upon the Fed-Ex man pulled over on the side of the gravel road, contemplating helping a goat that had its head and horns caught in the fence. He looked perplexed and out of his league, so I saved him from this battle of wills and told him I could get it. After cussing at the goat for a minute, he finally gave up the fight and allowed me to help him from his prison. I had to chase him a little way from the fence because just like any goat, he was mulling over another bite at the grass through the fence. They never learn! As he ran off down the line to find his flock, I realized that his flock was out on the gravel road. The Fed-Ex guy was long gone, and he had to have seen them as he drove down the road, so he must have learned to pick his battles quickly. One problem leads to another around here. Truly, a lesson I should have learned by now is that if they're not mine, ignore it and keep moving.

There was a gate near the goats, so I slowly drove around them and opened it. It was a rigged-up gate with panels wired on as extra protection against sneaky goats. It didn't have a chain or latch, just wire to close it. I got the goats in, and called my mother-in-law to let her know her goats had been out in case there was a hole in the fence that I hadn't noticed. Just so you know, with goats, there is never a hole in the fence. They magically get out even if the fence is ten feet high.

As she drove down, checking out the fence line, she found a straggler I hadn't noticed, so I opened the gate again. It went in and my mother-in-law decided to close the gate herself. I had wired it from a larger wire that held it to the post when I got there, but the wire was too thick for her and she couldn't quite get it around the fence wire and she didn't think that was enough anyway. She was getting irritated by the whole ordeal.

I'll describe my mother-in-law for a moment so you understand. If something bad could happen, she's already imagined it. While she was trying to wire the gate with the one large wire, she was probably picturing the wire falling off, the goats stampeding out, invading a neighbor's farm, making it to the nearest highway, causing a horrific crash that would be on the nightly news involving a school bus full of children, as the goats continue on their rampage throughout the country and finally assassinate Miss Universe. I'm 99% sure this is how her mind works. So, instead of wiring the fence with the large wire once, she pulled off a thinner, longer wire and started wiring the gate shut, not in just one place, but all over. Think of a slinky after a baby has played with it for about 30 minutes. That's what the wire looked like wrapped around the gate.

It took a while, of course, to create this artistic expression of anger, and the whole time I was thinking, "My father-in-law is going to get PO'ed when he tries to get in this gate."

He would have no idea where to start. Then the genius idea dawned on me: If I did this to John, he'd get so flustered, he'd put a good latch on it just to avoid the confrontation it would start to discuss how to wire a gate. He would know that it would never go his way, and it would be easier just to make the gate easy to open and close, rather than have this conversation. I generally don't complain to him about these kinds of things (I just vent on my blog), but he knows that if he complains to me about how I would handle his rigged up farm problems, I'd get the upper hand easily by arguing, "I can't live like this."

Remember, I've used this once when the insulation wasn't all finished in our construction zone/house, and I was freezing to death. Out of fear that I would move to a completed home and he wouldn't have his dinner every night, he put up all the insulation while I was at work the next day. I'm pretty sure I could use the fear of starvation against him anytime I wanted.

At that moment, as I pictured my father-in-law's expression when he would eventually try to open this gate, I decided I was going to use this technique to get things done around here. I just need to create a cluster... excuse me, a circus to get the ball rolling. I'm starting small with things like feeding the chickens.

I can hear it now…

"You didn't get the watering jug tightened and it all spilled out, and the feed should go in the feeder, not in a pile on the ground. You left the door open too and the chickens are wandering everywhere."

"Oh, well, I'll do better next time," I'd say, hiding a grin, knowing that he would do it instead.

"Don't worry about it, I'll do it next time."

"Really? I can help as soon as I make dinner."

"No, they all died from dehydration, so we'll have to wait until I get some more."

Ugh! This would be my luck. So maybe I won't start this experiment with the chickens.

I'd really like to use this technique on his Festiva (keep reading to learn about the widely popular farm vehicle of choice around here), but it will look suspicious if something happens to it under my watch because I generally avoid it like the plague and would walk five miles to town rather than drive it. I'll start small. Either way, my mother-in-law is a genius. Not all young women can say this. I'm lucky to have another desperate farm wife nearby to teach me exactly how a strong marriage is built - most certainly with fencing wire and bad language.

Life Quote: If you don't want to be asked to do something twice, do it wrong the first time. ~ John

NEW YEAR'S LIST / FARM YEAR'S LIST

Every New Year's Day, like most people that are unrealistically restarting the clock, I think that I need to have a to-do list for all of these tasks that I would like done around the house and farm, just to be prepared in case it ever happens. This list would be helpful after I throw a little trickery at my husband to get something done, such as the "do it wrong" method like my mother-in-law showed me or the "throw a hissy fit" method that I have perfected over the years. Like all of my to-do lists, it will be absolutely impossible to complete these endeavors, but since I wrote it with a wonderful cyan colored gel pen, it feels possible. I will not vow to lose weight because I have every intention of cooking with lard for every meal. I will not vow to exercise more because, well, because I don't want to. I will not vow to read more because I already kind of read a lot more than the average person by listening to audiobooks while I clean, so basically, I don't have time to read more. These are the things I will vow to do, and maybe succeed in completing one:

1.) Get duct work put in for central heating and air when my husband is at the sale barn for the afternoon.
2.) Put tin on the sides of the haybarn (and unlike my husband's tin that he put on the garage, make sure the tin isn't multiple shades of one color).
3.) Train Donnie, the Great Pyrenees, to be petted with minimal trips to the emergency room. He's not a human lover.
4.) Slowly, without my husband realizing what's happened until it's too late, send one useless car/truck/unidentified object at a time to the junkyard.
5.) Find the game cameras that the hunters put up and moon each one, just for the fun of it.
6.) Get rid of the black snake that hibernates under the woodpile and comes out whenever it's warm to hang above the front door or curl up in the sun right on the front step.
7.) Level out the yard so we don't randomly fall into giant sinkholes and so the pool will stay upright. Does anyone else have to use a ratchet strap to keep their pool from sliding away?
8.) Or get a net to catch any kid that gets washed away when the pool leans too far to one side.
9.) Put a railing on the deck, you know, so people feel safe to sit up there.
10.) Get rid of my phone because Trivia Crack is really lessening my ability to clean my house.
11.) Spend some quality time with my husband, showing him how to fold towels so they'll fit correctly in the cabinet and how to stack dishes to fit more in the drain.
12.) Teach my husband replacement words when he gets angry at the cows like "turd," "ornery," or even "jerk." Anything is better than what my youngest son has learned to yell at the stuffed cows in his toybox. My son's got a worse potty mouth than Pearl from the Will Ferrell rent videos. Look that up if you've never seen it.
13.) Pave the entire 2000-foot driveway with heat so I never have to

worry about being trapped or getting brain damage from the pot holes.

14.) Clean my house from top to bottom, organizing everything, so it looks somewhat like a normal house, minus paint and a ceiling in most rooms.

15.) Put a GPS device on every tool my husband owns. When they are lost, I can guarantee that 20% will be found in the grass surrounding our house, 20% will be at the in-laws, and the other 60% will be in one of his vehicles. Absolutely none of them will be in the house, so there is no reason to ask me 30 times if I've seen the wire cutters.

16.) Put a GPS on my heavy-duty kitchen scissors for those times that my husband can't find the wire cutters.

Wish me luck!

Life Quote: Well, my day has already gone to s#$. ~ Me, after my purple gel pen gave out as I was writing my to-do list at 7:00 A.M.*

Other General Irritations

You're probably thinking, "Her poor husband. She complains a lot," and you would be right.

∞

One thing I have learned since moving to the farm is that everything is done a little differently around here. I was raised to do things one way and my husband was raised to do things in the complete opposite way, so we're making do. I make fun of him, and he makes fun of me, and we make do. I think I'm right, and he thinks he's right, and we make do. Thankfully, we agree on politics, religion, and that Indian food is awesome, so we're set. Our differences in lifestyle irritate me, but he enjoys it because he goes out of his way to irritate me even more. After years of irritation, I'm getting worn down and the irritations are becoming normal. Well, not normal, but I'm just too lazy to argue, and that just might be a very important key in a marriage.

∞

A HILLBILLY'S CHRISTMAS DECORATIONS

Since our first Christmas together, my husband and I have argued about Christmas. He has no Christmas spirit. He's Ebenezer Scrooge.

He asks, "Why spend money on a tree when there are perfectly good ones outside?"

Or "Why wrap presents when they're already wrapped in the Wal-Mart bag they came in?"

I have an abundance of Christmas spirit, but I completely get where he's coming from, and I wish I was more like that. He grew up with a family that was milking dairy cows twice a day. They didn't have the time or energy to wrap a present. If it was a really special gift it was wrapped in the comics, and they were given mostly practical gifts, which as an adult, I have come to absolutely love. If it saves me time shopping, then yes, please, I want that as a gift.

A go-to gift for my husband: Carhartt jeans because he needs new jeans all the time. A go-to gift for me: sweet wines. It's practical because it saves me a trip to the store that I know I'll have to take during the holidays. A go-to gift for my boys: underwear because a boy mom regularly throws out underwear. Boys are disgusting.

I grew up in a household that had time to enjoy our presents so I didn't receive many practical gifts. It was all sporting equipment, electronics, and tickets to exciting events. The present was about the excitement and presentation, so when my husband suggests plastic bag holiday wrapping, my philosophy, of course, is different.

My reply - "Because that's ugly," and a very disdainful, "What is wrong with you?"

I know, that seems harsh, but the very idea of not wrapping a present is like nails on a chalkboard to my perfectionist soul. Wrapping a present with perfect corners and invisible tape is like a drug to my poor anxious nerves. I have problems.

To prepare our first Christmas tree, I spent a lot of money. I bought white lights galore, red and gold ribbons to hang from the top, and fake poinsettias and holly. I purchased antique-looking glass ornaments, different sized glittery and shiny ornaments in gold and red, and homemade clay snowmen in top hats. I had to have a sturdy tree to support these heavy decorations, so a beautiful, lush green Scotch pine would be the only answer.

No way, no how would I be running around this farm to find a cedar tree. This division of opinion surfaced as our first seasonal argument.

"You know, a cedar tree is free and smells great," my husband would suggest before I headed out for my perfect tree.

"Okay, Charlie Brown," I'd respond because he was not ruining my Christmas. I didn't let him stop me and found an amazing tree that was tall, round, and completely without a bald spot.

As I started to decorate my newly purchased and freshly cut tree, my husband asked where he could put the two ornaments he owned. They were items from his childhood that had special meaning. I looked them over and told him he couldn't; they didn't match.

Needless to say, he was offended. He took this as a gesture of war and kept sneaking them on when I wasn't looking.

In my defense, he had other options. I bought a three-foot fake tree that all the mismatched ornaments could go on. Even I had personal ornaments that couldn't go on the big tree. To appease him, I even bought multi-colored lights (which I detest), but he wasn't having it. He still complained. I relented a little. His grandma had given him one of the ornaments, so I told him he could put it on, but it had to hang inside the tree, and I showed him how to put ornaments inside and outside the tree to fill it (I could be a professional decorator, or professional procrastinator because I really had more important things to do). I would not allow the other one because it looked like it came from a box of Cheerios.

Besides this one mismatched ornament, my tree was perfect. It looked like it belonged in a department store. It was tall and fat, covered with red and gold. I topped it with a ribbon creation that took me three hours to make. The electric meter was spinning out of control with the amount of lights twinkling on this one tree. The presents were wrapped in matching red and gold paper with beautifully decorated ribbons. I was pretty proud of myself. My husband was disgusted. It was a little much for our tiny trailer. For the next month we'd have to turn sideways to get from the living room to the kitchen without disturbing the tree.

My husband continued to complain about the tree, asking things like, "When we have kids, are you going to let them put their homemade decorations on the tree?" trying to lay a guilt trip on me so I'd relent to his Cheerios ornament. At that time, we didn't have children so I was absolutely sure I could withstand a little one's whining and begging, something I later learned is a talent I do not possess, but I had no problem telling my husband no. He had his little tree. That was that! Then he got his revenge, and got it in a way that used my own techniques against me.

I came home one Saturday night from my second job as a

waitress. At the time I was teaching high school English full time and waitressing on whatever day I had to spare. Didn't you know, every teacher has a second job? As I walked in the door, completely exhausted, the tree lights were already plugged in, but my husband was not at home. It put a smile on my face to walk into the house with my beautiful tree all lit up. I went to the refrigerator to get something to drink, and also grabbed a cup to fill the tree stand with water. I watered the tree, then sat in the recliner, resting my feet, drink in hand, and stretched out to admire my tree.

That's when I noticed it. There were more decorations, but they hadn't been as noticeable as his other attempts at sabotage because these new ornaments matched. I got out of the recliner and took a closer look. He had used my advice and layered the new decorations inside the tree. I had to get pretty close to realize what exactly the new decorations were, but I was fuming by the time I saw the deer and its large rack, printed on a gold and red Stag beer can.

As it turns out, while I was at work, my husband and one of his friends thought it would be funny to get a case of Stag, drink the nasty stuff, and decorate my tree. My husband's only defense was, "They matched, didn't they?" He did such a good job of hiding them in the tree, and my tree was just so darn big, that it took me a few days before I found the last of the twelve cans, yes, all twelve, in my tree. They had a good evening, probably followed by a rough morning.

Now, the years have worn me down and by the time Christmas rolls around, I'm too tired to go cut down a tree at a cute Christmas tree farm, especially now that I have kids. Some people have lots of energy and capture some great Instagram moments at the tree farm, drinking cider, riding on the tractor trailer after cutting down their tree. Not me! Not anymore! Farm life and being the mother of two boys has taken a lot (all) of the perfectionist out of me.

I head out to get a lop-sided, half brown cedar tree just 50 feet from the house, so I might as well let him put on any ornament that he wants. We'll put on multi-colored lights and Cheerios ornaments. I've got a couple of pink ornaments that really clash with my red and gold. I've got some tiny purple ornaments that I purchased for a classroom display. I might as well throw those on too. While we're at it, we should just go all out. I'll decorate the tree and he can alternate drinking Stag and Busch Light, and we'll have red, gold, blue, and silver. The next thing you know, he'll be stringing popcorn on the tree, and I'll be at the mall, crying my eyes out in front of a Dillard's professionally decorated ten-foot tree.

Life Quote: Oh Christmas tree, oh Christmas tree, why did he defile you? Oh Christmas tree, oh Christmas tree, Stag beer's stench is like poo poo. ~ Me, I just made that up.

I call this artistic piece of work *Sweet Revenge.*

WHIRRA, WHIRRA, DEEP FREEZE

One evening, while discussing my blog *Desperate Farmwives*, the inspiration behind this book, my husband bluntly asked me with a hopeful tone in his voice, "Do you think you can keep going with these stories forever?"

My response was, "Of course, you do something ass-backwards every day, so I've got plenty of material."

I even have a journal of ideas that I've been adding to for years. My sister-in-law also texts me the asinine hillbilly events that happen at her house, so I have plenty to write about. I don't have to wait for the funny stories to happen. They're everywhere and mostly don't seem funny at the time. It's the little everyday things that start adding up to make me crazy. Even though this journal list is pretty darn long, I'm always thinking of new ideas or quotes.

My former students probably remember the easiest assignment they were ever given, the brainstorming bubble charts. I love brainstorming with a bubble chart. Put a topic in the center and related ideas on the outside. Then you can continue to branch off with more bubbles as details, ideas, and questions come to mind. Bubble charts are the kind of stretching that I can't hurt myself doing – stretching of the brain. I was creating one of these bubble charts to come up with more ideas for my journal when an idea came to me that had alluded me until that point, even though it was right in my face every day. As I tapped my pencil on the table a noise started driving me nuts. Sitting in the living room during my son's nap time, I stared at a bubble impatiently.

It was quiet except for a whirra-whirra-whirra. Should I write a story about the sheepdogs, the awful driveway, the clothesline in the house, whirra-whirra-whirra, the redneck cable, cow patties, whirra-whirra-whirra? Ugh, that sound was driving me nuts. Then it dawned on me; what does every desperate farm wife have? A gigantic deep freeze.

That electricity-sucking sound from the deep freeze may drive me nuts, but on a sleepless night, when the sound stops, I'm thrown into an all-out massive panic, throwing open the door to make sure half a cow, a pig, and our chickens aren't defrosting to a mess. It is a huge advantage of living on a farm to have all that meat at your disposal, but the very thought of having to frantically move it at 3:00 A.M. makes me ill.

Growing up, my family had a stand-up freezer with very little in it. I have no idea why we really needed that much space when we lived a half-mile from the grocery store and meat locker. It was stocked with a few T.V. dinners, popsicles, and way far in the back behind a bag of hash browns was a bottle of Kessler. Hey, I said we lived in town, not that we were civilized.

Our deep freeze is probably older than the one my parents had when I was younger. Obviously, you've figured out that it hums, but it also looks awful from its age. It's enormous too. We basically had to plan our house around how much space this thing would take up.

And that humming is a sure sign of the amount of electricity it's pulling, according to our electric bill. Despite all that, it's more reliable than a new deep freeze, so very necessary (I crossed my fingers and knocked on an exposed stud as I wrote that, so I'm pretty sure I didn't just jinx myself).

Even though the deep freeze has its purpose, it has acquired many other side jobs that can be quite annoying. These are all reasons why people put the deep freeze in the garage.

First, it's become the other countertop. Most people would think, "great, more space," but we really don't need another spot to pile things on. We are one pile away from being clinically diagnosed with hoarding. I would use the freezer to prepare dinner, but my husband has piled the following items on it: tools, chainsaws, a cattle scale, a lamb, a tire, fence posts, car parts, calf bottles, and colostrum.

Ladies, if you don't know what that last thing is, do not ask my husband or you will have an inappropriate, uncomfortable conversation where he compares you to a cow, but he works those comparisons in all the time, not because he's rude, but I think because that's all he knows about the female gender.

When this extra countertop is completely full is when I realize I've forgotten something inside it. Instead of cleaning it off, we tend to do a balancing act where my husband will lift the door and hold down anything breakable, while I reach in and try to find something by touch. We break two to three dishes because of this every week.

The second job it has acquired is a jungle gym. It used to serve as a good place for my husband and I to hide things from our sons, but we didn't realize that it would backfire on us. When our oldest, Aiden, would see a soda in our hands, he'd throw a huge fit because he wanted some, but as soon as we sat it on the freezer, too high and too far back for his eyesight, it was like it never existed.

We go with the child-rearing method "Do as I say, not as I do." After that we started hiding annoying toys, candy, and prunes there. Aiden's favorite snack was prunes, so it was completely necessary to find a good hiding spot for them, to save him a mad dash for the potty. Sadly, this hiding spot didn't last for long because they both quickly became climbers.

Now it's become the jungle gym, and we had no idea that we were encouraging that by putting things just out of their reach. I guess all furniture become a jungle gym at one time or another when you have children, but this is just out of hand. The youngest, Owen, loves to pull something up to it, climb up, and wait for us to walk by so he can leap out at us when we least expect it. It's dangerous and scares the pee out of me. He's a monster.

The third job the deep freeze has taken on is the official hiding spot for all our silverware. Things tend to fall behind it by either rolling away from us or sliding off as we try to squeeze an arm through to get a package of meat after the top is completely covered with dinner prep. Every time it happens, I stand there and think, I really should get that out, but it's a hard task to complete.

Since it's ridiculously heavy, I only clean behind it every five years. We were moving the last time, so I had to anyway, but it's time for me to do it again. I've found lots of things behind that deep freeze, so it's like winning the lottery, finding silverware, plates, Christmas decorations, a credit card, and literally the lottery, a small fortune of $40 in change.

It's a big massive pain in the butt, causing me worry, sucking up electricity, and eating my car keys, but I truly do not know the heartache of a real grocery bill. My Aldi cart is filled with rice, potatoes, lots of fruits and vegetables, and an ungodly amount of pickled things. I shop like a vegetarian and come home and eat like T-Rex. My husband always says the freezer is getting low on meat (even though it's not even close), and he'll then schedule something to get butchered when we have plenty already. At that point, I'm left with two options: take the great amount of time to reorganize the freezer and find space for chickens, a pig, or God forbid a whole cow, or throw it all on top and eat pork for a month or two until we can reach other meats. Since the latter is basically what we do every time - gorging ourselves on one meat until we can't stand it anymore - I don't see a need to change it up now.

Life Quote: We're meatavours. ~ Our response when eating dinner with vegetarians, whom I had happened to make vegetarian options for, and then they still ate our food, so either my vegetarian cooking was terrible, or they weren't really vegetarians.

GARDENING: THE BANE OF MY EXISTENCE

For years I have been determined to have an amazing garden. My mother and father, who are divorced, seem to have a competition going on with who gets the first tomato, but they find out by asking my brother or me for the juicy details. I guess this is where I got my need to garden, but sadly, I didn't pay a lot of attention when I was younger to earn the title of green thumb. I remember helping a couple of times in the garden. One time stands out painfully since I picked habanero peppers without gloves on and paid for it after touching my face, getting habanero in my eyes, and also spending the evening with my hands in cold water to ease the burn. Either that memorable experience blocked out all the other times I helped, or that was one of the few times I helped, so my mother naturally didn't warn me on purpose. Honestly, I don't have an urge to garden either, other than that I really, really want tomatoes, lots of tomatoes, on the ready when I'm hungry.

My first garden somewhat failed for lack of experience and effort, but I live on a farm, and isn't a garden what all farm wives do? I wasn't going to give up! The next garden was started too late, which then was repeated for the next few years when I was a teacher. Springtime madness! Then I started getting my act together and had small success for a couple of years, but I had a kid, and my act fell apart, but at least it became a hilariously cute mess. As I was finally figuring it all out, we had an extremely wet summer, and no one had a great garden (except for my dad who worked some sort of sorcery which my mother absolutely hated).

After that wet year, I thought I was going to have an amazing garden. I was determined, but as always, time started slowly slipping away, so one weekend I went with the improvised, "get-r-done" approach to gardening and had the sore muscles and blisters to prove it.

That mess of a garden really started the year before. Our tiller broke, and my husband had the wonderfully economic idea of just letting the pigs till it up. Genius! Now let me tell you the downfalls to that plan:

1. They root and root and root with no particular plan, therefore, our garden is now like the rolling hills of Ireland (except nothing grows as well). They literally created a mountain range in my 10 by 20 garden.
2. Transporting them was a chore. It's a pretty short distance between the garden fence and the pig fence, so getting out the trailer seemed silly. My husband had to drag them by their back legs back to their pen. Many other options were tried until his back said, "No more!"
3. Pigs eat corn, corn from the co-op, and that corn has a small amount of cockle burrs in it, which then rudely multiply uncontrollably. When it was time to start cleaning up the garden, I spent multiple days just pulling up cockle burrs. It created a pretty large bonfire.

My advice: Just buy a new tiller.

After that learning experience, did we buy a tiller, you ask? No, we really never learn a lesson if it involves spending a dollar.

"I think we need to buy a tiller," I say to my husband over dinner.

"There's a tiller in the garage, it just needs a little work," he replies.

"Are you going to fix it?" I ask, "Because it's been in there broken for a few years."

"No," he says.

"Are you going to take it to a repair shop?" I ask.

"That's expensive," he says in disgust, "but maybe I'll get the pigs out again. That's free."

My husband was also trying to be helpful when he suggested laying out hay last year before planting to smother any weeds. He wanted to save me some time, which is so sweet of him, but instead of doing it with a plan he just threw a whole round bale in the garden. Our garden is not very big. One square bail might have done it. He didn't even really lay out the whole round bale either. It took a foot before I could get to any dirt for planting. I just started moving it out in handfuls because it was easier to pick up than to actually rake.

He then burned some of it off, along with all the grass in the yard and one of the posts at the top of the driveway, but we didn't need it anyway. I'm just glad the fire went that way instead of toward the house. Well, it would have solved our construction problem, but no, I digress and I do love my house, or what I picture it will be.

I raked off whatever hay was left in the garden and it was ready to till. He worked on the tiller to no avail. He asked his parents for their tiller, and what do you know, it wasn't working right either. We then borrowed his grandparents' tiller, which we promptly broke before we finished a row. I even suggested using the pigs again, as long as we didn't feed them in there, but I guess the idea of dragging them back and forth multiple times didn't appeal to my husband.

So, one weekend I decided it was time to just do it without tilling. I went out with a hoe and broke up the dirt in any place I wanted a plant. It was hard as a rock and it took a little water, some elbow grease, and some angry thoughts, but I got it done (with some serious blisters and a core workout that would create jealousy from any gym groupie). Most of my time was spent excavating little plastic dinosaurs that my son had planted weeks before in hopes of digging up fossils later. That was my own fault because at the time I saw it as a way to keep him busy so I could clear the garden, but I didn't think about the future, which would be him digging up all my plants to find his fossils.

I also caged the tomato plants ahead of time, which is a first. We usually wait until they are huge plants and it takes two of us to maneuver them into the cage without breaking the vines. My husband then suggested I cage everything, you know, to keep them safe from a four-year-old who never looks where he's going. We've had many a cherry tomato plant lose its life from the clodhopping of a little boy...may they rest in garden heaven. Both of my sons would obviously fall over the cages, but at least they won't step on the plants.

After spending hours in the garden that day, I went inside to relax and cool down. My back was sore, my hands hurt, and I was covered in sweat and dirt. I just lay on the floor and let the baby pinch and bite me as he crinkled up his nose at my stench. I was too tired to defend myself.

Then my husband came in and informed me that there was a rabbit hole in the garden with a whole nest of baby bunnies. I had somehow not noticed this.

I was unable to keep Peter Rabbit or his family out of my garden that year. Maybe next year I'll have a winning garden. I say that every year though. By taking it down a notch and starting with a few mineral buckets, I have forgone the dilemma of a whole plot. With just a few buckets, some corral poop, and a little attention, I now have more tomatoes than I've ever had. Using what we had on hand, a ton of buckets and a ton of poop, I am almost able to keep up with my salsa and bruschetta habits.

I would like a full garden one day though. I do not plan to do it myself, absolutely not. When I win the lottery, my gardener will do it for me while I read books and delegate, and then lead other farm wives to believe I have mastered the art, living the dream of an HGTV celebrity. Living the dream, people!

Life Quote: I had my first red tomato stolen right out of the garden today, dang hooligans. ~ My mom, as I sat completely stone-faced.

NOT MEANT FOR A SUBDIVISION

Mowing - springtime's gift to all people with OCD tendencies. For people with those tendencies such as myself, having a yard like mine can cause some serious headaches. I've written about this a couple of times. As a matter of fact, it was part of my very first blog and the intro to this book. The theme was basically that I was caving to the madness around here; well, really, that's plain as day in everything I write and this is further proof, but it will also show a progression of improvement with the different generations of wives in this family.

First of all, my sister-in-law once sent me a message explaining her predicament while mowing the lawn. It was basically a dangerous, tall grass scavenger hunt. She found multiple things hidden in the grass, all before they hit the mower blades, thankfully. The list included cow bones, old running shoes, a piece of a hairbrush, an extension cord, a hammer, and a machete. *A machete*! That must mean someone attempted to mow the grass old style when it was too long to use the mower and gave up. It is completely normal for our husbands to leave something like a machete in tall grass. There are no barefoot walks around here.

I have had the same problem a few times. Before we moved to our own personal construction zone heaven, we had a flat yard that was a breeze to mow, unless you waited to mow for months at a time. Lots of things would turn up in the tall grass and come shooting out of the lawn mower at 100 miles an hour. Car parts, cans, fence wires, leftover scrap electrical wire, and even fully functioning electrical wire that hadn't been buried yet. Not cool!

I sometimes think I should not have alerted my husband about my life insurance policy.

Once, my husband tried to brush hog the backyard when it got really out of hand and he ended up hitting a stump and breaking the mower. I then decided to weedeat the whole thing and found that bees had created a nest out of the old grass that had been matted on the ground below the tall weedy grass currently looming over the yard. It involved some tricky business to get out of that one, but I only got stung once.

Now we're getting a little better about keeping up with it, even though it doesn't look like it. Kids want to play outside all day! If you let them play outside all day in tall grass, they come back in with chigger bites everywhere and you have to spend all day applying Caladryl and yelling at them to stop scratching, and explain to them that no, their wiener won't explode, but they have to stop scratching it so the swelling will go down.

You will then find yourself on the phone, while the kids watch a cartoon, calling your pediatrician's helpline and whispering to the nurse on call, "I told them it won't explode, but it looks like it's going to explode. It won't explode, will it?"

To save time in the long run from nursing, yelling, and embarrassing scratching episodes in public, lawnmowing is a must, especially when you're a little house surrounded by wilderness trying to take back its rightful place.

The mower we currently use has a bent blade so one side has a down-to-the-ground cut, while the other side has a nonexistent cut. I pick up the yard frequently to save my husband the guilt of running over a plastic dinosaur which has been left in the yard because he'd never be forgiven.

There is hope for the future though. In 30 years, I hope to be like my mother-in-law, the proud owner of a half decent mower that takes care of business. My father-in-law complains that their yard is getting bigger and bigger. My grandmother-in-law had it even better. She complained to me at one time that, "Fred does a terrible job (of mowing), just terrible. He misses that spot and that spot. He doesn't even try."

Then she just had someone else mow her lawn. If I just wait 55-60 years, I'll get someone else to mow my lawn too, and I don't mean some*thing* else like a flock of sheep. I mean a real person with the appropriate equipment.

Life Quote: It's a matter of taste. ~ My husband when I ask him how he can stand tall grass.

THE WOOD STOVE

When I win the lottery, and yes, I said when, not if, the first thing I'd probably do before hiring my gardener and personal assistant would be to install a central heating and air system. Yeah, we're stuck in the middle ages over here. The air conditioner doesn't really matter to me; I can generally survive in the heat, but I become a lazy sissy when it starts to get cold.

As the daylight disappears, my husband gets out the headlamp to continue his chores into the dark evenings, and I snuggle on the couch and say I'm going to fold laundry, but then I just snuggle in the laundry and fall asleep.

"Shhhhh," my youngest will say when John comes in, "We read Mommy stories and put her to bed," as he's surrounded by every snack cake he could find in the cabinet during his time of free reign.

During cold weather, my body starts to go into hibernation mode and all I want to do is sleep. I am physically pained by shivering, and it brings out a toddler's tantrum in me. I've been known to stomp my feet and start screaming bloody murder just from five minutes in the cold. I lose patience easily if that ice-cold feeling creeps into my toes. However, the worst part of winter, what annoys me the most - and the sheer thought of it makes me grit my teeth - is the wood stove.

I did not grow up with a wood stove. My brother and I fought for the best spot around the floor furnace, the spot that could keep you warm and still in sight of the TV. We occasionally burned our arms if we nodded off and leaned in too far, but at least all we had to do was turn a dial to warm it up. We even melted our shoes on that furnace and probably could have roasted smores if we would have been thinking and not sleeping. It was dangerous, but it sure was warm.

Most farm families I know have moved into the modern ages, but not us. Some have wood stoves just for show, but rarely used, or they have an outdoor stove. The ones that I am most jealous of have fake fireplaces and the best geothermal systems money can buy because they've cleared every last tree from their farms. Sorry, I do know the importance of trees, but man, I'd cut every single one down to keep it a steady 75 degrees in this house. I'm selfish in this one way (well, probably other ways too).

With a wood stove, it's a ridiculous amount of prep work and comes with all kinds of pitfalls that most townies don't enjoy. On the first day that it's up and running, my nose gets all dry and stuffy feeling, and that special treat won't go away for the remainder of the winter, no matter what size industrial humidifier I purchase. The wood stove will also start smoking in the house a few times a year, no matter how well we manage it, and undoubtedly it will happen in the middle of the night. I'll wake up choking and slowly realize the haze around me is not the slow, groggy process of waking up, but the smoke spreading, ever so lightly a foot or two from the ceilings. Then I'll have to go around the house with fans to get all the smoke out, Febreze everything so we don't smell like hippies or chain smokers, and deal with a scratchy throat for the next week or two. Also, there is a danger of losing skin or smashing fingernails when I'm loading it. All winter long I usually have one fingernail discolored by bruising and two or three places where the skin has been scraped off as I threw a piece of wood into the stove. Basically, my hands look like a mangled mess all winter.

They are also mangled from splitting the wood, but that's another very long, aggravating, my-husband-should-just-do-it story. What I'm really trying to say is, my husband is the biggest part of the problem with the woodstove. I'm almost 100% certain that he uses it to drive me nuts and makes it into a game for his enjoyment. Being the efficient tightwad that he is, he sells the firewood he cuts from the farm. He's making money while clearing the land for more cattle to graze, but I'm sure this is not really the main reason he goes to all the trouble. He likes to see me scramble after the initial, well-cut load is gone. He starts me out with the best wood, pieces small and dry enough that it's easy to start a fire, but once that's gone, it's a free-for-all. I have to steal it from his piles. I'm like a squirrel hoarding nuts, but I'm hoarding small pieces of wood that I can handle on my own with minor injuries and any cedar since it burns extremely hot.

I then burn it as soon as I find it, and if there's more than the stove will allow, I bring it inside the house because the unspoken agreement is that once it's inside, it's mine. I also spread it out throughout the woodpile, so it's not as noticeable. If I could get enough at once, I would even hide it under our bed, but it hasn't come to that yet. When the kids are napping and my husband is gone, I check the trailers that are being loaded and the ground around the splitter for more treasures to add to my hoard. When the snow starts and the temperature really drops, that's when this squirrel gets crazy and the game becomes a showdown. I'll usually snap and start yelling about the lack of good wood to burn as I'm trying to split a dense, 100-year-old, yet still green, stump. At this point I'll try to lock my husband out until he just brings the good stuff to me.

Instead, what I usually get are huge chunks of slow, low burning wood with a bundle of bail wrap. That gets the fire roaring to the point that parts of the wood stove start to turn red and sparks fly out of the chimney. No kindling is needed to start this fire, just a fast hand so you don't get burned as you throw a match on the combustible bail wrap that explodes in a nanosecond. A weird pungent smell then wafts through the house so it is obviously chemically poisoning us. When it's January and zero degrees outside, even I won't complain.

I understand that wood is cheap heat, and when you are grazing cattle, it needs to be cleared for grass anyway, but a push of a button seems so wonderful and magical, and just plain common sense. There wasn't any prep work to heating the house in my formative years, at least that I had to be a part of. No one ever asked me to climb into the crawl space under the house and light the pilot light, so it's hard to change my impulsive behavior now. All I needed to do was move the dial to 85° when my parents weren't looking. One day my husband will come home to a work crew installing the finest ductwork and industrial size heating and cooling system that ten scrapped Festivas (I promise, I'm getting to the Festivas) can afford, but until that day, I'll get my revenge by going through three times as much wood as anyone else who buys it.

It is nice to be able to have it 85° without that bill, and yes, I literally mean 85° because there's no in between.

As I've said before in a shrill annoying voice to my husband, "It's either Siberia or the tropics in here!"

But I do love the tropics!

Maybe a wood stove and a furnace would be the better bet. That way I could hide the furnace in a closet and it could be my little secret. He'll never look there. If he has ever looked in the one finished closet in our basement, I would have heard about it, or literally heard it as all the boxes I've shoved in there tumble on top of him. If the furnace made some noise when it kicked on, it wouldn't matter; it might just be the humming of the freezer to him. I'll just keep the radio on at all times.

I'll compromise to that extent, but it is absolutely necessary to install a furnace, if not for the times the fire is out after a long absence, definitely for the in between times when the weather can't figure itself out. After all, we live in Missouri, so it's not narrowed down to spring and fall. It could be January and 70° out.

When you have a wood stove and nothing else to warm your house, this in between time is a little torturous. It feels good outside with light sweaters on, but inside it tends to stay a bit cold. Or it's amazingly hot, or it's cold again, Missouri, Missouri, Missouri. So, do you or don't you? Do you start up the wood stove, which will have you down to your undies in no time and will get smoky because it's not cold enough outside to draw the smoke out of the pipe quickly? Do you wait and pile on clothes? I will pile on clothes, but there are a few other little tricks that I'll do to keep the house warm (when my husband's not around).

If you're the one paying the electric bill, these ideas probably aren't for you.

We have one space heater that we keep in our bathroom. No one wants to get naked or sit on a toilet in a cold house. Sitting on a really cold toilet really brings out the tortured screams in any hot-blooded human. In the dead of winter when the temperature is really cold, we plan our bathroom trips by turning on the heater and shutting the door for a few minutes before we attempt to shower or go number two. We tend to stay in there for much longer than necessary as well. It's a relaxing little sauna with a crate of books and magazines. It's a great hiding place for nerds like us, if only the locks weren't so old fashioned. A three-year-old can figure them out, but as all moms know, even if there is a bank vault door in your bathroom, they'd still get in and have an eye-to-eye serious conversation just when the coffee has kicked in.

When my husband's away and not available to give me that disapproving look that means, "Ahhhh...the electric bill," I'll carry the space heater to whatever room I'm occupying and set it on high. As soon as I hear a vehicle pull in the drive, I grab the heater and try to rush it back to the bathroom without severely burning myself. Sadly, I get the evil eye quite often because he tends to throw it in neutral and coast down the driveway. He's trying to catch me in the act of wasting electricity, and he's pretty good at it (because I'm a master at wasting electricity, if I must say so myself).

He also follows me around the house and turns off the lights behind me and glares at me as I look through the refrigerator for a snack, but it doesn't irritate me at all.

I also unapologetically do a large amount of long-term oven cooking during these cold days. Preheating extremely early is a must, all while leaving the oven slightly open, and I will sometimes postheat as well. These are meatloaf, casserole, roast kind of days. The longer the cooking time, the better. Our Dutch oven gets a workout during the fall.

"That smells awesome!" my husband exclaims over the cola pot roast or roasted chicken after coming in from a hard day's work.

"Just for you, Babe!" I say as I open the oven to check the food (to let the heat out) for the millionth time.

I should really take up baking, but I hate baking, so this is the time where I might take the lazy route and buy a cake mix. It's an inexpensive excuse to turn the oven on for 20-22 minutes at the coldest time of the day.

My sister-in-law is also not a baker, or a cook, but she has been blessed with a husband who is. Even though she doesn't know how to turn on the oven (Just kidding Jessica, but really, do you know how?), she came up with her own way of heating her tiny cabin during this in between weather time. When they lived in their cute little first home, the dryer became king. It was a time in her life when the laundry got done frequently, well, up to the point of drying, but who actually folds their laundry. The dryer was a great heat source, and she said it felt awesome to jump in some warm sweatpants.

I would use this as a heat source as well, but since my dryer came from the neighbor's garage sale for $5, it's only dependable for air, not heat, but it's better than the previous $10 dryer. It almost caught the house on fire. That's too much heat. I can do without that.

Life Quote: If I have to go back to teaching teenagers, I'm getting a huge loan, finishing the house, buying a new car, and living comfortably and beautifully. ~ Me, and this is the only way you can get me back in a classroom because teaching is hard on your soul and your skin.

THE PLAGUE IS UPON US: ASIAN LADY BEETLES

When it gets warm in our home, a monstrosity called an Asian lady beetle descends upon us. This happens for two reasons: 1.) our house is an incredibly open construction zone and 2.) they can get into anything, a half-done construction, an old construction, a new completed construction, and a lock box with a million-dollar seal on it. Because I can keep it very warm in our house because of the wood stove, these Asian lady beetles never seem to have a specific life cycle. They live forever.

I have spent weeks, and seasons, trying to do one thing...kill lady beetles. They go by many names including Asian lady bugs, orange lady bugs, stinky lady bugs, harmonia axyridis, and the plague that the Department of Ag inflicted on us. These bugs are a menace, one more aspect of farm life that I just can't stand, and they are driving me completely insane. These are not to be confused with the greenish Japanese beetles which have most recently afflicted us in the MidWest. Although equally menacing, they stay outside.

I'm not sure if these ladybug imposters are more common out in the country, but they must be because the people that complain about them the most are people that live out of town, so if you have no idea what I'm talking about, can I come live with you? I love to do laundry, my kids are really cute, and I think I'm a pretty darn good cook. Think about it.

I've heard that these bugs have two very active seasons during a year, but I'm thinking that that's only true in their original habitat because I've seen these monsters for six months in a row. When it gets really cold, they seem to disappear, but since a Missouri winter can sometimes be a piece of cake, they won't ever die. On every somewhat warm day, they start creeping around, attacking our windows. Then, the warmer it gets, the more aggressive they become.

I'd stand just inside the door with my son on a day 55 degrees or higher and give him the pep talk:

"Alright, now let's beat those bugs. I want to see you run to the car with everything you've got. Don't waste your time swatting or dodging; that only encourages them. Just run little man, run like you've never run before!"

Then I'd open the door, yell, "RUN, RUN, RUN!" as he was distracted by the cat, or the woodpile/activity center, or just his imagination, which left me carrying a baby and at least three bags, as I try to close the door, all while being surrounded by those nasty lady beetles.

Rule of the wise: Keep your mouth shut, eyes squinted, and pray they don't fly in your ear.

Now this has become my mission in life: How do I kill them? I know they kill other bugs that eat plants, that's the whole reason they were released in the U.S., but it's too late to have any reasoning for this. Anytime I go out and feel a slight tickle on my neck or arm, I start doing a little crazy dance thinking one is on me.

Now that's nothing new to the average Wal-Mart observer, but when people are on a mission in Aldi, they really do not like to wait behind you while you block a whole aisle trying to dig in your clothes to find what you thought was a lady beetle in your bra. I have almost taken a sip of coffee to look down and find a lady beetle floating in there, just staring up at me in triumph. One has flown into my mouth when I was outside hanging clothes on the line. That's my happy place, and those nasty bugs have taken it from me.

I've tried to just get rid of them. I've vacuumed them up to find that they just come back to life after the original shock, but not until they've sprayed their nasty stink. For those of you who haven't been blessed with Asian lady beetles, they have a distinctive odor to combat predators, a pungent, grassy kind of smell. It's gross anyway I describe it. I've put out sticky traps to see if they'll fly to them, which they do, but not in the desired number. Then I started using the lightly covered sticky trap as a bug broom. Once there are a few on it, you can swipe it across a covered window and catch more without the trap sticking to the window. It's disheartening though because after swiping a whole window and catching a hundred or more on the sticky trap, just as many or more will appear within minutes.

It's completely horrifying.

I've spent a lot of time on the internet trying to find solutions. I've read about little yellow bags that attract them and trap them once they're inside, but even though they are trapped, you are still attracting ten times as many toward your home, so those don't have great reviews. One post said to soak a cedar log in water for 24 hours and use the water to spray all over your yard. Supposedly, the bugs are detracted by the cedar oil that is now in the water. The post said they won't even go near cut cedar, but we've got a small stack outside the house in the woodpile and they have no problem crawling over it compared to the other wood, so I didn't even bother trying that. The proof is in the pudding and you will not trap me into another DIY, Pinterest.

Another post said that you should mix Dawn dishwashing liquid and water and spray that all over your yard. The author of the post said they are detracted by the smell. I thought I'd test it out in a small area first. Our windows are covered with the beetles when it's sunny out, so I covered a rag in dish soap, wiped it over one window, and let it dry. I kept it pretty soapy so the smell would stick around. Honestly, it worked somewhat. I'd say that it's 50% less covered than the other windows, but when 200 lady beetles are diminished to 100 lady beetles, it really doesn't impress me. I'm sure it only eliminates the weak so the stronger ones can breed even more beetles for the next extinction. I'm looking for mass annihilation.

So I spend my free time coming up with concoctions to scare away these lady beetles. I dream of going on *Shark Tank* with my idea. The sharks, of course, won't get it. They've never been in this predicament, but the producers will save the day.

"Twitter in the MidWest is exploding about her idea. Move her on, give her money. The tightwads of America want this product!" They'll be screaming through their earpieces.

I won't be there for the Sharks though. I'll be presenting to for all the Midwesterners out there who are at the end of their wits. The Sharks will listen to the earpiece gods and I'll be applauded and then sent on to QVC to become the next home shopping star. Maybe they'll make a movie about me like *Joy* but instead of Jennifer Lawrence playing the heroine, Amy Adams will get to play me and then be nominated for an Oscar after portraying the struggles I went through before achieving QVC success.

In reality, during my pitch on *Shark Tank,* I'll be interrupted by one of the sharks incredulously asking, "Wait, is this a real thing?"

Shark Tank isn't live and Twitter will never blow up for my pretend invention.

Yes, Sharks, this is a thing, and cute little lady bugs are being ruined for a whole generation of kids.

As for now, I'm to the end of my rope. I'm going to take the yellow bag, go on a long hike, over the hills and through the woods to one of the neighbor's farms, hang it where it won't be noticeable, and walk away. If they are attracted to a neighbor's place, maybe they'll leave our house alone.

Life Quote: HSN might be your better bet. ~ My mother, and she would know.

HELOISE, HELP ME!

As I mentioned before, laundry is my happy place. I love sorting, hanging, and folding laundry, but the Asian lady beetles have ruined the experience from time to time. I've come a long way in the laundry business. When I started doing my husband's laundry as well as my own (he's in charge of the dishes), I was shocked at the amount of time I would spend trying to remove stains, but I quickly realized to give that up when I would never succeed. Instead, I have a whole outfit in hiding in case we are going somewhere in public. Obviously, I don't have to hide dress clothes. If those have to be worn, I'll have to force him. If we're going to the bank or on a very important date to the Mexican restaurant, he doesn't need dress clothes, but it would be nice if he had a t-shirt without streaks of grease or jeans without calf placenta stains.

I do have to keep a couple of pairs of jeans (one blue jean and one khaki-colored Carhartt) and two t-shirts hidden. These become too tempting for him to wear out and about while he's working, which means that they will be covered in cow poop or car grease within minutes of leaving the house. The hiding spots for these items change frequently because when he does find them, he'll keep going back to them when I'm not around, and I have to be around to tell him to take them off after an outing or he'll continue wearing them on his next chore or disastrous mechanical mission.

These are my questions to the experienced farm laundresses or launderers: Is it possible to get these stains out of clothes or am I the only lazy person around who doesn't even try? Do you have clean clothes hidden for your significant other to wear, or does your significant other have some shame and won't go out looking homeless without your help? Do they even get as dirty as my husband when they go out to work on a vehicle or to work cows?

I understand why there are more stains on my husband's clothes though. He has multiple vehicles that are hanging on by a thread, so they need lots of TLC, just another example that you have to spend money to make money, or in this case, you have to spend money to save money. Also, when you have the cows he buys, you need to spend more time working on them so that's more opportunity to get pooped on. He also insists on preg checking his own cows, and if you didn't know, they don't use a little stick and some pee like we do. They make disposable gloves that go all the way up someone's arm so they can stick their arm up the cow's back end to feel for a calf. I'm assuming that cows really like my veterinarian sister-in-law's small arms, and I'm hoping that one of my husband's buddies doesn't check his own cows. His arms are huge, no... gigantic. That's just not nice. Anywho, when you stick your arm in there, it's not coming out without some poop, and most of the time, it's not just a little poop. It's shooting out, just adding more disgusting laundry to my already very large pile. Then I'll have green poop stains splattered all over the jeans, making spot treating miserable, and a t-shirt with one sleeve stained completely green. Yuck!

Needless to say, OxiClean does nothing for it. I need to invest in a power washer.

Not that I really want to add work to my growing list, but if anyone has any suggestions on how to get those stains out, please let me know. I'm not going to get them all, but once in a while my husband finds the hidden clean clothes and ruins them in minutes. I'd like an alternative to buying a-whole-nother set of jeans. Or if you'd just like to do my laundry, that would be even better.

Life Quote: When in doubt, throw it out. ~ Me, that's how I feel about his clothes.

THE TENNIS SHOE ROTATION

Farm laundry can be pretty bad, but I've learned that I can hide it fairly easy. I can keep it in the wicker laundry baskets, although wicker does not hold in smells. I can keep it in the washer and rewash it 50 times before I remember to hang it out. I can keep it on the clothesline multiple days in a row until I either need the space or it rains and I have to frantically take it all down before getting struck by lightning. I could hide it in the dryer, which is its only use because it can't dry anything. There are many options for hiding laundry, but I don't have many options for hiding shoes. They pile up just inside the front door and become less and less organized because none of us actually put them back on the shelves, mainly because there isn't enough shelf space for the large number of shoes we own, and there isn't a closet by the door in the basement dwelling in which we reside while the rest of the house is under construction.

You might be asking, "Why is this chapter referring to tennis shoes? Don't farmers wear boots. Cowboys boots, Muck boots, shitkickers, etc., etc., etc. That is the widely thought of assumption, but not here. Our boots stay pretty clean, but our tennis shoes (the preferred footwear) do not.

When I was ordering new tennis shoes online for my husband, I thought, "This is something that's got to be unique to us, and maybe a couple other cheap farmers." We have a process called "cheap shoe rotation."

We don't have a shoe fetish; we have a rotation.

I've heard of runners switching out shoes from running shoes to everyday shoes, but I wonder if other people living on a farm do what we do. It's based on the idea that you must keep something until it has 100% given up on you, so for a shoe, it must fall off your feet AND can't be put back together with duct tape or a glue gun (sometimes staples if you're desperate and have had a tetanus shot recently).

When my husband uses his shoe as a hand puppet with the toe as the mouth and mimes in a dorky voice, "Looks like I've got a problem," I know it's safe to throw it away and rotate him into a different pair.

The first thing you might ask as already mentioned is why we don't wear boots. We both have boots, but unless it's absolutely necessary, we avoid them. They are too expensive to replace over and over, they cause sweaty, stinky feet, they are hard to get off and on, and when you don't know what you'll be getting into (water, mud, poop, etc.), it saves a lot of time when you have multiple pairs of tennis shoes that you can slip off quickly, hose down, and put on the next pair. I say "we," but honestly, I mean "he." My boots are ten years old and they are just as shiny as the day I got them. I will fight, and whine, and blunder through farm chores with every fiber of my being.

The last farm chore I helped with was to simply stand in the driveway while he moved sheep in the hopes that they wouldn't run past me. To my credit, they didn't go around me because they were afraid. I couldn't even be trusted to simply sit there quietly because I turned on my smartphone and sang and danced around to Rita Ora's *I Will Never Let You Down* as the sheep started running back and forth frantically. I was bored and Rita Ora is just amazing. By the way, my shoes did get pretty dusty that day, but I think it was from my awesome dance moves and less about the sheep.

My husband is the one dealing with dirty footwear most days, minus hosing them down, but sometimes it's just easier to let them dry and beat the mud off. He just lets them dry with cow poop or not and wears them later. If my shoes get covered in cow poop, I take it as a sign that I've dealt with enough and stay inside to wash my shoes.

All joking aside, there really is a very specific rotation to tennis shoes on a farm if you are going to go that route instead of wearing something heavy duty. Tennis shoes can be categorized into three types: new tennis shoes, stained tennis shoes, and falling apart tennis shoes. I will now explain in great detail what you can do with your tennis shoes during their lifespan in each of these categories in case you feel like saving every pair of tennis shoe you've ever purchased.

This is not only giving you an insight into the strange things my husband does but a very weird insight into how my mind works.

Ahhhh, the smell of new tennis shoes. You better enjoy that smell because it doesn't last long around here. It's replaced by poop fairly quickly. These are not work shoes. They are reserved for going out in public, or if someone is coming over, and you want them to think that you aren't on the verge of destitution (or when the soles fall off the bottom rung tennis shoe, in which the rotation shifts and online ordering begins).

These new shoes must be put on in the car because there are too many obstacles from the front door to the nearest vehicle. It's not uncommon that we have to dodge a cow patty from the "lawn mowers," a mudslide from the last rainfall, or a toddler trying to see how far he can pee (my children really are heathens). These are all reasons my new tennis shoes get ruined, but also from being dragged into helping my husband without preparing, and they quickly get moved down to the slightly stained category if I can't OxiClean them fast enough. That's the second time I've mentioned OxiClean. Maybe there's an endorsement in my future.

My husband's brand-new tennis shoes get ruined because he puts them on for any job when I've forgotten to hide them after going out, or he wears them to the sale barn. In my opinion, the sale barn is not technically "going out" because it's just going from one stinky, dirty corral to another, but he wears them anyway and they always come back to be downgraded to the slightly stained category.

The slightly stained category is where most of my shoes stay. I don't wear them down as fast as my husband. His shoes stay in this category for a very short time. These shoes are for wearing out and about, if it's clear that you are working. When I get into an exercise kick, these are the shoes I'll wear, but that's not often. I used to buy my husband gray shoes, but since they end up brown by the time they get to the slightly stained category, I switched to a brown hiking shoe in the attempt to keep them looking new, which by no means works at all. Mud and cow poop do most of the damage once he's slipped past me in new shoes.

Unlike me, he never tries to wash them. He just leaves them out in the rain to get the chunks off or lets them dry and beats them together to get a wearable pair. They are cheap shoes, so they are going to fall apart quickly, but he doesn't do a whole lot to prevent them from falling apart at all.

I wear my falling apart shoes for mowing, weed eating, or severe muddy conditions. My husband wears his all the time, for anything unless he judges that it's too embarrassing, which isn't often enough. I have noticed a few times, when we've made trips to town together or when he's walking into the house after returning from a public location, that he's had on what looks like a half a shoe with a whole lot of sock showing. He really has no shame. I've recently caught myself picking my son up from school in my own ratty, poop-stained tennies. I'm slowly being drawn into the depths of degradation.

Another parent looked down at my feet but said nothing, and I conscientiously replied (and yes, this was a lie), "Oh, I was helping John move cows and I didn't want to get my good shoes dirty."

In reality, I wear those shoes all day unless I leave the property out of extreme precaution.

A time or two my husband's shoes have been moved down to the falling apart stage because he's left them outside and one of our dogs chewed one up and carried it away to be found at a later date. If you've ever heard the studies about moms having more of a home workload even if their spouses help around the house, this is a clear example. Who else would save a loner shoe in case a matching pair shows up or even thinks ahead and buys the same shoe for just this situation? Maybe just me, but the to-do lists a woman has going on in her head is what keeps the world going 'round.

Early on I learned that it would save lots of money if I bought him the same style shoe, so if one is missing, it could be saved for later to match another loner shoe. Sometimes animals may step on them and cause a rip. Most of the time it's the welder's fault, so says my husband. As he is welding, he'll look down and find sparks burning through the mesh material on top of his shoes, and occasionally, all the way through his socks. Folks, this is obviously a busy man if he doesn't even notice the smell of burning fabric. Of course, he notices burning flesh. Let's just hope that he never spills gas on his shoes, then decides to weld.

I just added a garage fire extinguisher to that mental to-do list.

As of now, the number of pairs of shoes I buy each year is still cheaper than any alternative. When he breaks a foot from not having his steel-toed boots on, that may change, but if it's just a broken toe, there's no need to bother a doctor. If you do see my husband out on the farm, or working on anything dirty off the farm, or even at the sale barn, you have authorization to confiscate any tennies that look too new for him. He definitely did not have permission to wear them. If he complains that he is now shoeless, give him some duct tape and tell him to go to town because that's all his worst shoes are anyway.

Life Quote: Super glue will get it done. ~ My husband, as he looks at the shreds left of his tennis shoe which has most certainly reached its last day of rotation.

WHERE AM I SUPPOSED TO PARK?

It is a daily struggle to live in a construction zone, and I'm sure if I write another book in ten years, it will be in the same state, so I better get used to it. I clean constantly, and it's still a mess. I often daydream about easily cleaning painted walls and using a Roomba without the fear of burning it up on chunks of sheetrock and plywood. There are always dangerous tools and materials which I'm hiding from my sons. Also, we live like sardines in the basement, storing everything that will eventually be spread out throughout two other floors. By the time we have the house done, I won't be able to carry things up two flights of stairs. I get winded even now! In the process of all this, most of the possessions that we thought we needed to save have broken.

We chose to live this way, which is the craziest part of it. Having a dream can lead to questionable decision making. We wanted to buy a farm, so we did, and we wanted to leave our options open to buy more land (maybe one day), so we decided to build our own home so we wouldn't be tied down by a home loan. Then, as we were on a roll at working on our house, inch by inch, I slammed the brakes on the gravy train of a teacher's salary (hahahahhahaha, that's funny, right there) and quit my job to be a self-sacrificing and fantastic stay-at-home mom (jokes on them because I'm just mediocre). So now, we really have to scrimp and save for each construction project.

My husband, so very meticulous, plans it all out. "It's the end of the month and we have about $10 left in our monthly budget for... what... maybe a small can of paint, a few outlet cov-"

"Wine!" I shout. "We need wine!"

Then we get three bottles of Aldi wine with change to spare.

A while ago my husband suggested we take a break from the house and build a garage with a loft to safely store some of our junk. Now, I know, this was a sneaky ploy to have a place to park his tractor, but I was so tired of piling box after box after box in every corner of the house that I quickly agreed. They were becoming a hazard. I'd take a quick trip to the bathroom and find my one-year-old son three-quarters of the way to the ceiling as the boxes gently swayed back and forth like something straight out of a cartoon. Also, with a garage, I'd have a place to park my car out of the winter elements and that was a plus.

In reality, do I get to park in the garage? Absolutely not.

Part of this is my fault. If the garage was attached to the house, I'd fight a bit more to get my car in there, but it was my idea to keep the garage separate, so the farm has taken full possession of it. I suggested a completely separate garage because I have a serious symmetry problem. I like things to be symmetrical, so adding a garage to the house would have sent me into a mental tailspin. If you took a picture of our house and folded it in half vertically, everything would match.

Elementary teachers - need a copy for math class? I'm your gal.

The only way I will allow a garage to be built onto the house now is if we added something else to the opposite side, or better yet, build a bat cave under the house that does not alter the aesthetic of the perfectly foldable picture. My car could enter the cave entrance down the hill from the house.

My husband does not even respond to that idea, yet he fills the new garage to the brink with all kinds of stuff. I was able to park in it for two weeks before I was getting edged out, inch by inch, without realizing it. One day I couldn't park all the way in and before I knew it, farm stuff took over my space completely. These are the items in the garage right now: a tractor, another deep freeze, a four-wheeler, a lawn mower, stacks of tires, three improvised workbenches, tools on anything but the workbenches, ladders on the ground, an auger wagon to store feed, and a welder in a wheelchair (my husband's inventive way to save time and his back). My husband's car is the size of a sardine can, so he should be able to pull in the garage with no problem, but he's left himself no room as well. His truck sits outside the garage or next to the house to fill any spot that might even serve as a windbreak, so I park in the drive like a common guest.

welder on wheels

Obviously, this garage has become "crap central." It's not all farm equipment. The loft has cleared a lot (but not enough) out of the house. We are hoarders, so the garage loft is where our

Rubbermaid crates end up to be forgotten. Even the stuff that should be in the loft gets crammed in the garage because the loft is full. It was jam-packed with stuff the day the last sheet of plywood went down on the floor. We basically have too much stuff, so I'll continue to scrape my windows on frosty mornings, or I'll drive the length of the driveway with one icy peephole to see through. Our driveway is very long, so by the time I make it to the end, I generally can see out of a basketball-sized clearing in the frost. And if it's really cold, and I'm just too lazy and cold to bare it, I'll pull my car off the driveway right up to the door and create my own special spot. It should have a sign posted: Reserved for Desperate Farmwives.

Life Quote: I think I need to build a lean-to on the shed. ~ My husband's solution to the overflowing garage.

A COUNTRY HALLOWEEN

I started this section out with a holiday, so I might as well wrap it up with another holiday. You'll find so many good examples of amazing autumn decorations in the country, but probably not at my house. As a child, my mother went **all out** for Halloween. We had lots of decorations. My friends always came over for a Halloween party, and my mother made her famous popcorn balls which even adults would trick-or-treat for (or send their kids to the door with a request for extras). It was a big deal. It was good ol' wholesome townie fun. Even throughout high school, we'd still have the party, watch a scary movie, and scare the little kids who were trick-or-treating by blending into the decorations. No kidding, we were just drinking soda. Caffeinated? Yes. Spiked? No. Well, everyone except the one person who told her mom she was going to my party and snuck out to the real party outside of town; then when she snuck back, we had to force feed her hot dog buns in a vain attempt to sober her up. Don't worry, her mom knows now.

Isn't that how it works? You wait 10 years, have a few glasses of wine with your friend and her mother because you're now adults and can drink their wine without stealing it. Then you tell on her for every time she snuck out or had too much to drink or went skinny dipping in her pond with….wait, I haven't shared that yet. I need to save it for the next time.

Anywho, so the love of decorating for Halloween has stuck with me, although I haven't really caught up with the new style of country motif decorations. I'm still in the 80's and 90's, when stuffing leaves from the yard into giant pumpkin bags and old clothes made all the best decorations, and I'm taking it to a new level.

On the other hand, my husband's family lived so far off the road, they didn't see the need to decorate, even though their driveway looked like the opening credits to a murder mystery. I saw this lack of enthusiasm as a challenge and decided to incorporate my holiday style into his life.

Our first year together was somewhat easy. It was all about dressing up and going to a party. He was not going to dress up, but getting him to go have a beer would never be a problem, and since I was the obligatory bar-hopping saloon girl our first Halloween together, he didn't necessarily need to dress up because he only needed to be a bar patron. Then, after I moved in with him, I decided to ease him into the Halloween spirit with just a few decorations, but he was disgusted about any time wasted on holidays and got a good laugh at my attempts. The cows knocked over my pumpkins, the real spider webs on the porch took over the fake ones I put up (so it was a little redundant), and the mums were really only there to draw attention downward from the giant missing section in the porch. It was not a success. Even though he did get a good laugh out of my first attempt, he really just complained, complained, complained.

Challenge accepted sir. I tried harder the next year. I decided we'd make pumpkin people and put them outside the gate (away from the cows). Then the same six people, four of them in-laws, could see them while driving down our gravel road. I came home from my Halloween shopping with a trunk full of pumpkins.

My husband rolled his eyes, and of course asked, "How much did you spend on pumpkins?"

I never answer those "how much" questions honestly. I bet he's asked me a thousand times how much my wedding dress cost and he still doesn't know. It costs a lot of money to have a revealing dress that actually only reveals what it's supposed to without any wardrobe malfunctions, so he should be happy that he enjoyed the view. Even if I said, "They just gave the pumpkins to me because I'm so super nice," he'd said, "You still wasted gas money."

When I explained to him the concept of pumpkin people, a Halloween tradition on our porch growing up, he was intrigued. "So they can do whatever?" he asked.

"Yep, whatever," I replied. "They can play dead, sit on hay bales and look pretty, do something frightening to freak people out, whatever."

So, our first set of pumpkin people sat in their lawn chairs drinking beer. My husband was bending to the new regime.

After that he generally agreed to help if the idea was good enough. He even went with me to pick out pumpkins. We'd go to Colvin's, the local pumpkin patch, and he'd stand around and act like I was a nut for being particular about pumpkin shape, size, and color. When the number of pumpkins would get out of hand, he'd insist on knowing where each one would go, so if I was going to pick out a lot, I needed a good idea to support my hoard of pumpkins, but I always had a game plan. I'd been wasting many a planning period searching *Country* magazine in the school library for ideas. This was before Pinterest made our idea search easy and our spare time scarce.

His favorite year was the year of the toilets. He owned a trailer park at the time and had a surplus of toilets for some reason. I constantly made fun of him for the amount of time he personally spent in the bathroom. What I didn't know at the time was that this is a very common male trait. He always said it was urgent, but then would spend 45 minutes in there, either reading from one of his many farm books or reading *The Grass Farmer* front to back. He still does this, and I think he just uses it as quiet time. I decided to use this as my theme. One pumpkin person was him, reading *The Grass Farmer,* and the other was me, reading *To Kill a Mockingbird.* The two neighbors and four in-laws thoroughly enjoyed it.

Since then we've moved, so we have a much wider audience on a state highway, but I try not to get too out of hand because we live on an accident-prone curve. The year my oldest son was born, we had a baby pumpkin person, and another year the little pumpkin boy was sitting on a potty even though the real boy was only interested in peeing anywhere he actually shouldn't at the time (and technically still today).

The year my second son was born, we had another cute one with mommy and daddy pumpkin people, holding a cute little pumpkin baby, while a toddler pumpkin boy was climbing over the fence behind us with a handsaw, and a sign next to him that read, "Toddler Terror…. Nightmare on Stroupe Street." The terror is very accurate. Any parent who has just added a second child to the mix and has seen their first little angel turn into a screaming demon in seconds can attest. My oldest boy took over last year and insisted on a dragon pumpkin design, so thank goodness for Pinterest. He's really into *Star Wars* now, so let's hope Pinterest can save the day again.

No matter what the design, I'll hear two things from my husband for certain:

1. This is ridiculous.

2. You spoil those boys.

He is right on both counts, but he does laugh every time he sees what new Halloween ideas I've come up with, but he does hate socializing, so he most certainly dislikes all the attention he gets in the grocery store now that people can see them from the highway and want to tell him how funny they are or give him ideas on what to do next. So it's a win-win for me!

Life Quote: I read it on the toilet. ~ My husband, any time my current reading selection disappears.

For
Sale

∞

Everything is for sale, right? For the right price, right? Well, this is my attempt to sell you something, especially if you have no intention of recommending this book to anyone else (I have to earn a living somehow). What better way to solve some of my problems than to sell off some of those general irritations I was just talking about, but we need to act fast before my husband gets a chance to sit on the toilet and read this book in entirety. Think of it as an infomercial on a Sunday afternoon, when they tell you that you only have five minutes to act fast and buy a self-cleaning litter box or an expandable/collapsible water hose.

By the way, both of those things are at your local supply store and on television *every* Sunday afternoon, but this sale of the random things in our yard or on our farm only lasts for the next 1-365 days. My husband will read the book in a day, but it might take him 365 days to remove it all, so act fast.

If you would like to buy anything listed for sale in this section, I'll make a deal, a very good deal. You can get any item half price, or you can trade with bottles of sweet white wine or an expandable/collapsible water hose.

∞

TIRES

I'm a hoarder. It's true. I've been this way since I was little. We went to a lot of fairs when I was young, like every weekend of the summer, so I acquired lots of carnival crap that would disintegrate under very little pressure, but I'd keep my foam walking lizards and rubber jewelry for as long as they were recognizable. Two or three times in my life I've had the time and energy to purge and I was depressed for weeks after, just thinking about all the perfectly good small squares of construction paper I threw away.

I'd lie in bed awake at night and calculate, "About 1,672 sit ups a day and I could have fit into those jeans again. I shouldn't have given up on them."

In some future rampage of spring cleaning, I really need to do something about the grocery bags, magazines, and "important" papers that really just need to be thrown away. What I really need is someone to force me to do it, but my husband is just as bad as me.

He has more t-shirts than you can find in the Hanes aisle at Wal-

Mart, yet only wears five of them. Technically more, but one is a plain gray Hanes t-shirt that he owns four of, but I can't tell the difference until they get a certain farm stain, and right now they are too new. The other shirt he wears is one of the many shirts my brother and sister-in-law have given him on their many traveling adventures, which has a PG-13 joke about camping and wieners on it. The rest are either too inappropriate to wear in public or too bright for him.

The particular PG-13 one is gray, of course, has an imprint of a camping stick figure near his campfire, and says "I went camping and burned my wiener in Cody, Wyoming."

Slightly inappropriate, but not nearly as bad as the rest.

My husband also seems to be a hoarder of empty oil jugs. For a normal person, that would mean a few jugs around the garage, but there are lots of motors and engines around this place, so that means we have jugs of every shape, size, and color strewn across our garage. These can even be recycled, but they end up in the garage forever until a particular windy storm and they get thrown about the field for me to slowly pick up as I find them in the tall grass.

Last, but not least, something I've seen many men do, especially on a farm - he is a hoarder of tires.

There are tire piles all over the place around here, all sizes. There's a stack of great big tires from one of the trucks blocking my parking spot right now, and I don't mean the garage parking spot. That's been gone for a while. I mean the parking spot that I made for myself just outside the garage. It's overflowing! There is another giant pile of smaller tires by the garden, cast offs from all the trailers and cars. Also, if you go for a walk, you could find random tires near tree or fence lines, exactly where they had been changed. I just don't understand where these tires come from. None of them are from my car. I take mine in for new tires, say goodbye to the old ones, and never see them again.

Not only does my husband pile up every tire that he finds, he also borrows tires. I've overheard phone calls with his dad as he has asked him, "Where's this watcha-ma-call-it?" and "Are the tires pretty good?" "I need to borrow them for a few hours to move this load of tires to another place on the farm." You never catch me calling someone to borrow tires. I can imagine the conversation.

"Hey Teri, what size tires do you have?"

"How am I supposed to know that?" would be her response.

"Check the tire wall."

"What?"

"Anyway, if they are 205/55R16, can I borrow one? My driver's side rear tire is bald, and I need to run to St. Louis. I'll bring it right back."

Pause.

"Call Grotjan's, fool!" Click.

In case you are reading this from a location 30 miles or more away, Grotjan's is the tire place. If I happened to call my sister-in-law Jessica with the same problem, she would most certainly say, "Oh no, they've gotten to you," and rush over with wine and Netflix to pull me out of it.

Also, those borrowed tires never get returned. They end up flat and added to the pile.

My husband has been looking up other uses for these tires at least, or that's what I thought. In *Ag Talk* or *Farm Show*, two of his daily reads, it mentioned making water tanks out of old tires, which he's already done. He is also planning to make a sandbox for our sons out of one. Then I realized these ideas were not minimizing our tire piles. He was getting these tires from somewhere else, but he added, "But they were free."

So I need to come up with an idea to get rid of these tires or make a use for them. I need a brainstorming bubble chart! I could start a tire museum. There's a museum for everything else in Missouri - dolls, hair, dogs - why not tires?

I should also try Pinterest. There's probably a tire house that I could build and then create my own office away from the house. Actually, my husband informed me that there is such a thing when I brought it up. I just need to read *Farm Show* more often. For right now, I'll just take an inventory, so let me know if you need any old balding tires. I'm sure I'll have exactly what you need.

I'm ready to made a deal!

Life Quote: I'll give it to you for free! ~ Me, about the tires, please take them, please!

FESTIVA

I cannot say that we have a junk yard...because a junk yard keeps all their vehicles in nice little rows and ours are scattered all over, basically hidden so I don't complain about them all the time. I would need a map to lead a buyer to a particular car or truck, a map that would have to be updated frequently. The legend on this map would need a special color or shape - a tin can perhaps - to indicate where a Festiva is located on the farm since that is the prominent hidden gem that can be found scattered throughout 150 acres. Festivas, of which there have been a lot of in our family history, have great gas mileage, are inexpensive to buy and/or repair, and have ruined my mental health for a while now.

One afternoon, after my kids and I were visiting with family all day and my husband spent all day at the sale barn, it was time for me to get to work (cleaning, writing, solving the world's problems, etc.). We decided that I would go home and he would stay with the kids at his family's house because it's just too dang hard to drag a toddler away from fun without leaving a trail of cupcakes to the car and locking him in.

When my husband finally arrived, the most logical thing to do was switch cars because the car seats were in my car.

But he drove the Festiva. Instead of the newer truck, or the older truck, or the other truck that has no real use, he chose to drive over in the Festiva. His family lives two miles from our house. It's not like he'd be saving a ton of gas, but I could possibly lose my life driving home in a tin can.

After a separate, disgraceful Festiva incident which I'll share later, I have refused to drive one of his Festivas anywhere. He's had multiple, and they've come in all colors, multi-colored too like the Christmas lights. Being the helpful and cheerful wife that I am, and since I just wanted to get home to some peace and quiet, I chose to be obliging and drove the Festiva home.

Before I left, I asked, "Any tricks with this car?"

There's always a trick with any vehicle he owns. Here are a few tricks from other former vehicles in his menagerie:

- leave the window down so you don't pass out from gas fumes
- push that button when you start it, but make sure the key is exactly right here (sparks may fly)
- put a bucket behind the seat if you want to reach the pedals
- the shaking stops between 52 and 54 MPH

This time he said, "Nothing much," and this is what nothing much actually means:

I left the house slowly but surely. I didn't kill it, but it did not accelerate. I backed up to turn around while my brother-in-law was getting something out of his car, and I was taking so long and revving up the engine so much, I think he was getting nervous that I was just going to plow right into him because he kept giving me side-eye as he dug around frantically for whatever it was he was looking for.

After backing down a hill, I finally shot out of the driveway, realizing the first problem. I couldn't get it to turn right as I left the driveway and almost plowed into the fence on the other side of the gravel road. I cleared it with an inch to spare.

I thought, "It needs some power steering fluid, but no, no, oh crap, it doesn't!"

I guess it just needed a little warm up because half way home it seemed like any little nudge and I'd be on the other side of the road. That was probably the 10 MPH wind picking it up and moving it though.

My husband also did not warn me of the decorative steering wheel cover that does not stay in position, so as I tried to correct myself on the gravel road, I almost created a new corral entrance for the neighbors as I tried to steer and the steering wheel cover slowly slid with my hands. At this time, I also realized that the brakes don't work, until they do, then the car stops as my body continues hurdling forward. I finally made it down the gravel but had a short stint on the highway ahead of me. When I pulled out onto the highway, I was all alone, so I could just sail home.

But no, that didn't work out either. It took so long to get going as this little tin can was putt-putting down the highway, sounding slightly like a chain-smoking bumble bee, that of course, a very large truck came barreling up behind me. Great! I was going to have to turn soon, with testy power steering and dangerous brakes.

I turned the blinker on and slowed down, but that truck kept on coming. Hmmm, he didn't mention a blinker being out, but I wouldn't suspect he would. That's not necessary on a vehicle that doesn't need an inspection for another year.

I made it though, refusing to slow down anymore, actually unable to because the brakes were scared as well. I flew into the driveway and made a quick 90 degree turn and still managed to down shift before I killed it. Winner winner, chicken dinner. I even opened and closed the gate without a problem. The problem did come though when the little Festiva with 12-inch tires met its driveway nemesis - the two-foot-deep mud hole.

I knew the pot hole was there, but I was on an "I survived" high and just completely forgot that this little car might not take the pothole well.

BANG!

CLUNK!

"Darn it!" I yelled, crescendoing into a Hulk Smash kind of yell.

That's when I killed it. I rocked back and forth trying to get it out, I reversed into more rocky mud, and spent a minute trying the old standby - gun it out of pure anger and hope that it just magically digs its way out. Then I remembered what I was driving, a lightweight Festiva. My six-month-old at the time weighed more than that car. Yes, as my husband always said, my baby looked like he was on full feed, but I could still lift him. I gingerly got out of the car and picked up the Festiva, moving it to dry ground.

No, not really, it slammed down pretty hard and just bounced right out, but I may have hallucinated that bit about lifting it because I smacked my head really hard on the roof of the car as I bounced back out of the pothole. I left brain cells there that day. Hopefully I didn't leave any Festiva parts behind (but really, I don't care). I made it home with a throbbing headache, but thankfully I still had my life. I thought about parking the Festiva downhill toward the woods just in case the brakes decided to give out but thought better of it. It would have been awesome for a minute or two but Festivas never die. If the brakes did "magically" give out, it would get beat up, lose the mirrors, shatter the windshield, and my husband would still drive it.

Soon after that incident, I was given a ray of hope. My mother-in-law was stuck with my father-in-law's Festiva, like I said, it's a family thing, and it broke down at the grocery store. He had her nice car and she was stuck with the old beater. By the end of the night they both owned nice cars. I don't know what went down for that to happen, maybe some cursing, stamping of feet, a baseball bat to the hood, no telling, but it happened. I have a dream that one day, I too, will have a husband that can no longer steal my dependable car to get around. He too shall have his own dependable car, not by choice, but from manipulation, yelling, guilt, and a little fear.

Life Quote: When I get my license, I want to drive the Festiva. ~ Says only a 5-year-old, my 5-year-old.

Even little superheroes can lift a Festiva with their pinkie!

THE REAL REASON I HOLD A GRUDGE AGAINST THE FESTIVA

Festivas really are inexpensive vehicles, let's make that clear, and if you choose to come by my house and purchase one, you might as well buy two, you know, to save money because you'll undoubtably need a $10 part or two right away. As I said before, blinkers may need fixing. I'll just give you a backup Festiva for $10, or two for the price of one. You can't beat that.

I'm trying to be objective, and my beef really isn't with the Ford corporation, more with the way my husband hangs on to a vehicle long past its prime or refuses to fix the simplest of items on a vehicle if it works in some fashion or is not intrinsically necessary to the actual driving process. That might also mean it's illegal, but that doesn't matter to him until it's time to get an inspection, and even then, he only does the bare minimum.

It was at one of these inspections that the Festiva (I'm not sure which one because they were all multi-colored, mostly red, so basically the model as a whole) lost my respect forever. My husband left the car at the mechanic's shop overnight. We'd driven into town the night before, dropped it off, and with the help of Mexican food at a local restaurant (probably more so the margarita), he tricked me into picking it up the next day. Nothing can mollify me into a happy, helpful person more than a full belly and margaritas.

"Thanks for helping me drop it off this evening," he said smiling.

"Slurp," I reply, also smiling.

"Do you want more chips?" he asked.

"Sluuurrp!" That means yes in margarita talk.

"Your margarita is low. Would you like another?" he asked, and the tequila has already diminished my judgment.

"Sluuurrp!!!" Note the extra exclamation marks.

"Would you pick up the Festiva tomorrow?"

"Slllluuurrrppp!" That's a "sure thing and would you like fries with that?"

I agreed readily as I slurped down my fishbowl-sized slushy (that's the only way to get them, am I right?), then went home to dream of a never-ending river of frozen peach/mango margarita at my disposal at all times. I woke up with a headache, knowing this was a mistake.

My brother-in-law, who lives just down the road, drove me in to town and dropped me off, and although I really wanted him to drive it back, I didn't want to put him out any more than he already had been, and I didn't want to look like a wussy girl who can't drive a stick shift. I most certainly can. I've driven around Ireland with a stick shift without ever killing it (only occasionally slapping the door looking for the stick when I'd temporarily switch back to an American car in my mind). It's a vehicle of my husband's with which I have a problem. None of them work right and they all have little tricks. Like before, I had not been prepared for the little tricks on this car.

I paid for the inspection, not entirely sure if it passed or not, just saying thanks as I nervously wondered how I was going to get this car out of the tiny parking lot. It was a busy afternoon and cars were everywhere. I was very afraid that I would manage to hit someone - no, not really - I was very afraid of looking like an ass as I tried to get this beater out of the lot.

I got in, and yes, this was the one which needed a bucket behind it so the front driver's seat wouldn't slide back too far, so I had to get right back out and put the bucket, which thankfully was in the back seat, in its spot so I could reach the pedals. This car had a button start, and the button mounting was hanging off the dash for some reason, probably a small but necessary repair my husband made without completely putting things back together afterward. As I stepped on the clutch and then pushed the button, it made an awful noise as if I'd started a car which was already started, you know, that high-pitched grinding sound. It was loud and everyone turned to look. My face turned red, and I quickly put my head down in the hopes that no one from this town of 1,700 would know who I was. It's hard to do that when your now retired high school math teacher is at the gas pump, your Great Aunt Louise is at the counter paying for her tire change, and your church minister is walking by at that moment.

After a few curse words, I tried it again, and again, it made that awful noise. Ugh! A couple of the guys in the shop now looked up from their work to check out the commotion coming from the tin can in the parking lot, the one they all probably rock-paper-scissored to get out of inspecting since it would no doubt be a very questionable inspection indeed. I tried it one more time, and as it squealed again, the local funny man who likes to hang out at the shop jumped through the door, right in front of the Festiva, crouched over like he was going to take a look at the front of the car, and instead, in very elaborate motions, moved his right arm as if he was cranking the car, like it was an old Model-T.

I was horrified and everyone in the lot had a good laugh. I was so horrified that I kind of threw a tantrum in the car, banging on the clutch and beating on the ignition switch, so of course, it magically started. Turns out the trick was that the clutch could only be half way down while the button was being pushed in half way.

COMPLETE RIDICULOUSNESS!!!

I drove home in indescribable embarrassment. One of those moments when you replay it over and over and plot revenge. When my husband returned home, he got an earful. He loves to tell this story to this day, which shows his lack of shame. It was his car - he should be embarrassed. Nope, he enjoys seeing the flush of anger and humiliation that washes over my face every time he hits the punchline.

Life Quote - &#$ &^%*! ^&*@ @#*& @&%$! *@&$ #@&*& @$# *&^#!!!! ~ *The gist of what he heard that night when he came home. Sometimes you just need to let it alllll out.*

TRUCKS, OTHER THINGS WITH MOTORS, AND RANDOM CRAP

Many, many, many other things are sitting around this farm which were once stored/hidden away for the purpose of creating some cool, helpful equipment my husband read about in *Farm Show* magazine, a publication that makes impressive farm equipment MacGyver-style, with whatever is lying around, fencing wire, and a combustion engine to make it dangerous if possible.

Conversations start with me saying, "What's that?"

He responds with, "Well, it's going to be a…"

Big things are planned for those piles that disappear behind tall grass and thorn trees.

Honestly, there is no story of how the other items around here accumulated because there is no rhyme or reason to it and, for most of these items, I really have no idea how they got here. They just appeared in the back of one of his $500 truck purchases as one owner decided to pawn off all kinds of large metal objects on the new owner of said truck. So, I'm going to make a list and if you want anything, just let me know. Remember, I will make trades in equivalent quantities of sweet white wine. I'll even take sweet red wines as well. Or margaritas, or the tequila with which to make margaritas. I'm not picky, just don't send anything fancy. I won't know what to do with it. I prefer quantity over quality, and there isn't anything here that requires an expensive trade.

To the highest bidder:

1. Utility trailer - A perfect place for mice and snakes to nest. It also holds lots of tools if you're brave enough to reach in between the reptile and rodent inhabitants.
2. Every washer and dryer we've ever owned, which are plenty, because when you buy them for $5 a pop, they aren't a lifetime investment.
3. A stock trailer with something wrong with the axle - I'm not sure what. I'll confess, I zone out of a lot of conversations about farm stuff.
4. Scrap metal – I probably shouldn't list that since we're in a rural area where thieves steal copper right off a house (but it would be cool if they took a little bit at a time, and just left a bottle of white wine in the mailbox).
5. A broken down three-wheeler, mower, and some type of farm equipment - don't know what it is, and yes, it's very common farm equipment. If you'd like to know the names, order, and birthdates of Henry VIII's wives, I could tell you that, but I have no capacity for farm equipment names or purposes.
6. Small feed bins (maybe the many broken ones could make a whole) - I would also take a trade on these small bins for a larger bin, about 14-18 feet in diameter, one that I can create a cool Pinterest project for my own office, my own little she-shed. I would even be willing to make the feed bin bar and invite you over for drinks. You should look that up – it's

super cute!

Wait, realization here, *Farm Show* is farmer Pinterest. Maybe instead of a sale, we both need DIY therapy, focusing on those who collect the items, but never create the final product. That is a serious breakthrough, but I might leave this topic alone for now. I have great plans for the cabinet doors, small chunks of discarded 2x4's, and multiple full boxes of baby food jars.

Life Quote: Did you throw ___________ (insert junk) away? ~ My husband, all the time.

Animals with Personality or Personality Disorders

∞

If you haven't figured it out yet because I avoid chores like the plague, I do really live on a farm, but technically speaking it's a ranch, but no one around here calls their land full of livestock a ranch. Around here, if you live on many acres, you live on a farm, and if you do anything with those acres - crops, livestock, or rent it out - you're a farmer. On our farm we've had many different animals, and when I say different, I don't mean variety, I mean different stages of weird or crazy. The cows, which have animal majority on the farm, are fairly boring. They mind their own business, eat grass, and poop in the driveway, so there's not much to tell about them.

One dairy cow, Star, was the farm superstar. Everyone had his or her picture taken on Star (which you probably noticed in the cover pages). She was very tame and didn't seem to mind being climbed on, so any new member of the family or visiting friend from college had to get his or her picture taken with Star. We also had a cow that hated me personally. She would go berserk any time I was around. My husband was mystified as to why she didn't like me, but it was just easier for him if I wasn't around for chores. Ahem...she was paid well for that service to me.

Cows may not give us too many stories, but the other animals around here have kept us on our toes. We have had many cats and dogs, a few of which were strays. We've had a few pigs and lots of sheep when my husband thinks they're worth the hassle, which is most of the time since they're the cleanup crew of the farm, a job no one else really wants to do. I like to say that each memorable animal had personality, but some of them may have had more of a disorder, or it could have been enforced from the chaos they were surrounded by. Nature vs. Nurture, the age-old question of if it's our fault that our children (or animals) act so terrible in public.

∞

DONNIE AND LESTER

Snowfall gets a varied reaction in our house. When we wake up to a new snow, my sons squeal, beg to be let out of the house to roll in it, and then demand an 8 A.M. grape snow slushy and chocolate snow ice cream. Since we're in Missouri, most of the time it quickly melts into a muddy mess so all I hear for the rest of the day are angry pouts. My husband becomes a cussing monster because he will have to clear some roads because of that side job that many farmers have around here. I just cry because even if I do keep it 80 degrees in the house, it's hard to pretend we're living it up in Barbados when our very large front windows display the opposite of tropical weather. My sons, of course, are happy and demand that I get out the snow gear for a torturing, 30 minutes in the cold. They get pretty excited, but the happiest creatures on this farm are the two Great Pyrenees that we own, bouncing around like two Chihuahuas, even though the rest of the year they move their 60-pound bodies at a snail's pace.

The dogs' names are Donnie and Lester. We got Donnie when my husband first bought some sheep, to protect them from coyotes.

Donnie was paired with Marie. I often name our feed animals with funny names too: The Supremes, Ham and Bacon, Pork and Beans, and Devil Cow have been some of the chosen (to supply our freezer). Marie the dog was the star, of course, so she ran off to join the circus. We got Lester to keep Donnie company.

Yes, Lester is female. It was the one shot I gave my husband at naming an animal, and he chose Lester from an inappropriate family joke that I can't tell here. He no longer gets to name anything except our children, and really, I manipulate that situation to get what I want. I was once a teacher, so the rules have been that I get to nix any name that would remind me of a problem student (as if he knows my students' names).

"William?"

"Nope, mouthy."

"Eric?"

"Nope, never turned in his homework."

"Peter?"

"Nope, nose picker."

I just kept that up until he said one that I liked. I can be more carefree with farm animal names though - no long-lost nose picker labels to worry about.

Donnie and Lester basically hate it here. They were not made for Missouri weather, but I feel for them because neither was I. They are big fluffy dogs so summertime really is hell to them. Even winter can anger them because one day they are frolicking in the snow and the next day they are dealing with a swift weather change. It could be 70 degrees outside and all their built-up fur becomes a furnace. During the summer we cannot grow grass in our yard because they scratch the ground for cooler earth and lay in it for a while until it heats up and they'll find a new spot. Our yard has mange. They lay around all day panting like they're on the verge of heat stroke, but when other dogs would jump in a pond to cool down, they would look on in disgust. With all that hair, they'd probably just sink.

When the first snow comes, we finally get to see some personality in these dogs. Their bodies finally get to a normal temperature and they're like a kid on caffeine. Lester will jump around and roll in the snow like she's having some sort of fit, but if dogs have a smile, there's definitely a smile on her face. I've only seen her move that fast once during the summer, when she was "playfully" terrorizing our chickens. A couple of chickens didn't get the memo and died of shock. One wintry morning, Lester really wanted to play. I kept pushing her away as I loaded my car to head to work because she has been known to leave giant slobber marks on my clothes.

"No, Lester! Don't get me dirty," I said as I threw a bone across the yard to distract her.

She chased me down the driveway without finding the bone. The snow was melting and our driveway was turning into a mud mush. It's like Lester knew this was it, that her favorite part of winter was disappearing, and she needed to get out as much energy as possible. As I was trying to open the gate with one hand and using the other to hold Lester a few inches away from my khakis, Lester jumped up on me thinking it was a game, leaving two large paw prints on my upper back (she's a very big dog), almost knocking me over.

"Lester! You're a demon," I said as I got back into the car to turn around, already feeling the wet mud seeping through my new pink cardigan (Teacher Attire 101).

Lester jumped around like she'd won the game. If dogs could talk, she'd be shouting, "I know, I know!"

I had to go back to the house, change my clothes, and soak the cardigan I had on to remove the massive monster prints. I should have just accepted the slobber marks across my butt.

Donnie would never do that to me, but that's just because he'd rather rip my face off. He was bred and trained to be a sheep dog, so he doesn't like anything else. I've only been within five feet of him.

He will run off if anyone gets closer, with the exception of my mother-in-law. He really hates her for some reason and will get a wee bit too close for comfort to show his displeasure.

One afternoon, I was sitting at the table in our basement, which is a walkout with giant windows, when I heard Donnie start to bark. In the middle of the day, that usually means someone is pulling up the driveway but that someone was actually already here. From the corner of my eye, I saw a flash of white hair flying off the retaining wall into the yard, and quickly realized that it wasn't the dog; it was my mother-in-law diving from the top and scrambling to the back door as Donnie barked at her from the driveway.

It was a slow-motion long jump.

She exercises regularly, so thankfully she wasn't hurt, and it was more like a quick, high-intensity workout, but she was pretty mad. For some reason Donnie prefers to be extra aggressive toward her. I think it's because instead of yelling at him, she automatically runs, so we're trying to teach her to scare him, but I think it might be too late as he now knows who has the upper hand.

My husband tried putting a collar on him once by tricking him into the cattle trailer. That was the closest Donnie has been to a human, and he did not like it. My husband was afraid he'd lose his hand, so he gave up on the collar for a minute and thought he'd bring food to the trailer to lure Donnie closer. When he went back, Donnie was gone, and we had to assume that he was nimble enough to jump up to the openings of the trailer, which are pretty high up, and shimmy out. As Donnie watched from the trees, hiding away but out in the open enough to let us know he'd still like his dinner, my husband took this with relief. I figure, if we really need to catch him, we can drug his food or tranquilize him with a dart gun.

Donnie is here for a purpose though. He's not here to make friends. He looks at Lester in disgust when she falls in front of her human for a belly rub. She wants attention just like any other dog and will demand that she gets it with a gentle nudge or a large muddy paw print. Donnie would love that, but he knows he has a job to do. If we start messing with his sheep, he gets pretty ticked off, but we've learned that he is actually just scared. If we yell at him to go away, he does, in a hurry. I just hope that he's not so easily persuaded by coyotes. When we yell at him, he literally runs off with his tail between his legs.

Then we get the sad face, as if he's saying, "I just want to be loved and no one understands me."

Sorry Donnie, I understand that you have a bark that's bigger than your bite, yet I still value my face.

Donnie and Lester get pretty bummed out when we hit a warm streak and the snow melts, which is usually shortly after its brief accumulation. They slowly mope up and down the driveway, waiting for someone or something to harass. When it finally sinks in that the snow is not coming back for a while, they'll go on about their usual business: eating everyone's dog food in the mile radius.

Life Quote: I'm not getting out of the car if Donnie is around. ~ My mother-in-law, from that day on.

DEER SEASON

Boom! I duck and hide behind some laundry that I'm hanging outside. Then I remember what time of year it is, go inside, get my bright orange shirt, and continue hanging out the clothes so they can get somewhat dry in this winter-like November weather and pray that no one shoots me.

Deer season is upon us.

Our family is not a bunch of hunting enthusiasts. My husband would like to consider himself a gun enthusiast if I'd let him get more, but he used to sleepwalk quite frequently, so I think the best policy is to keep fewer guns and keep them closer to *my* reach. He can complete numerous tasks while sleeping, and I'm sure firing a gun would be quite simple while sleeping. I'd rather not be the topic of a Dateline episode so I'll eliminate any dangers to my life (especially since I embarrass him quite frequently in this book).

Being a collector of guns is one thing, but hunting is completely different, requiring skills that we do not possess. That skill is not aim. We have great aim. We practice every day. When one of us isn't paying attention, the other stalks through the house and beams the other with my son's soft toy footballs, baseballs, and a monkey slingshot I brought back from a conference. We also do this to my son when we are too tired to chase him. I do not particularly like guns, but anytime I shoot one, I have amazing aim, but that's because I believe, and my son also says so, I'm a beast at anything I do.

The skill that we do not possess, which is paramount for hunting, is patience. Neither one of us is willing to sit in the cold and just wait. We'd get cranky just thinking about the things we could be getting done. We wouldn't notice one deer all day, imagining the work just piling up back home, but I bet we'd read a whole *Time* magazine and a book about cows or the Tudor court, depending on which one of us you're picturing. We'd eat every single snack we brought with us (about four meals worth) and then we'd sleep. We were not made to sit still, at least not without a T.V. in front of us.

Because of our inability to sit for more than five minutes before falling asleep, other people come over and hunt on the farm. Usually it's someone we know, so it's not anything to worry about, but one year no one asked, and the day before deer season someone who was hunting nearby asked my husband if he could hunt on our property as well. My husband's first impression of this man was that he seemed to be an arrogant jerk, so of course, his answer was, "You'll have to ask my wife."

Yes, thank you, your five months pregnant wife, who is still getting sick all the time and has dragon-fire heartburn, really wants to deal with this jerk face.

If you were thinking the animal with personality was going to be a deer in this story, nope. With every ounce of sarcasm and eye-rolling that I can muster, this man was the animal with a "personality."

So, the hunter came to me, and before he really introduced himself, he made a snide comment about our house.

"You live here?" he asked in a shocked tone.

"Yes, we are building as we live in the basement," I said calmly.

"You all should just hire someone to finish it," he said as he looked around in disgust.

If I really had dragon-fire heartburn, this would have been a perfect time to singe the rest of the hair off his balding head.

Instead, I replied, "What do you want?" in a tone so he'd hopefully understand that I didn't much care for him.

"Well sweetheart…"

I threw up a little in my mouth at this point.

He continued to ask if he could hunt on the farm, which I basically said no to at first, based on his '50's era attitude toward women, but he then offered money. We usually had a paying hunter at that time of the year, so I thought since that was not in our budget, I better think about it. Also, at that point in my pregnancy, I was sure the baby was a demon baby and I'd die in childbirth. I thought I should save money for my own extravagant New Orleans style funeral, so I haggled with him for a few minutes until we came up with a deal.

I was very confident in this deal until my husband told me what he'd talked to this turd about. My deal with the hunter was based on acres and men, which would have been four or five guys, but he told my husband fewer than he told me, so I knew right away he was going to swindle me.

So of course, the next morning, I got up at the butt crack of dawn, did my morning retching, and armed myself with saltines and Sprite. I went to the construction zone upstairs and sat in the dark with my binoculars so I could count how many guys got out when they arrived. Time rolled by and the sun came up - no one parked where we had discussed.

Unfortunately, instead of driving over, they had walked to their spots from the other neighboring farm. He was one step ahead of me, and I was not about to go out there and check it out. He was sketchy. He would have definitely shot me or at least shot near me just to make a comment about silly women and how I should go back to my house and cook something.

When he did come back to the house, he paid exactly what I thought he would - less than what we agreed.

When I questioned him, he had the excuse that only one of them had actually come over. Naturally, I was a little snippy with him. I should have been excited with anything since this was extra money that I had not planned on, but it was the principle of the matter, and this guy was a jerkface. I really wanted to put him in his place, but he was much more practiced at this than I was. He's obviously been a sneaky jerkface all his life. With every comment I made, he had another sweetly-coated condescending one for me.

A few days later after he'd packed everything up at the neighbor's farm, he saw me returning from work. I was at the end of the drive, checking the mail and collecting what was left of the Halloween decorations (yes, it was the middle of November). I wasn't fast enough before he jumped in his truck and drove over, catching me as I was trying to waddle back to my car.

"Hey sweetie!" he said as he rolled down the window.

I did not reply.

"I talked to your husband today and asked about next year, but he said I'd need to ask the Mrs. again."

He said it in a very patronizing tone. I wanted to say to him, in explanation, "My husband does not need my permission, he just can't say no to people and needs me to be the jerk once in a while," but I knew this guy would use that information against me and wriggle his way back next year. I only use this information sparingly, like when I want a Coke in a glass bottle from town, insulation in the **entire** house, or a two-week vacation in Ireland.

"So little lady…"

The way he said it made me want to give him a quick smack and remind him of why I'm the boss, but he just kept right on with an answer.

"I'll stop by next year before the season starts and we'll work out a deal."

As if I had said yes. ANIMAL!

"Here's some deer sausage." He handed me a bag and gestured like he was ready to leave.

I was inflamed. I hadn't even said yes and he was going to bulldoze me.

I snatched the bag. Remember, at this point I had a fire monster in my belly and I would never pass up a snack anyway, and I said gleefully, "Naaah, we'll have someone else hunt here next year."

"I'll pay more or stay on just this side of your farm if that's…."

"Nope, just a friend that gets full reign for FREE!" I said as I walked back to the car. Technically, I said free like I was singing it, you know, just like Oprah.

As I was shutting the door he was still saying, "Okay, I'll check with you next year."

I spent a whole year coming up with some man-hating comments for him, but he gained his senses and never did ask again, or maybe he asked my husband and he decided to tell him no so I'd stop raving about it. Now we have nice people hunting on the farm. I wear my giant orange t-shirt with leggings because I'm a cross between an always flexible ninja and a lazy mom. My sons have bright orange hats on even though we have no plans to hang out outside. We just make quick trips to the clothesline to get the frozen clothes off before the sun goes down and wait for the new, very polite hunter who is forever welcome on our farm to let us know what he's tagged.

I've had very nice conversations with the new hunter about kids, being a stay-at-home mom, being a former teacher (the same as his wife), and about teenagers (his warnings to me about what I'm in for). I've even helped him load a deer once that was just too big to get alone because I'm a beast, remember. This very nice man also sends us a smoked Christmas turkey every year as well.

When he's done hunting on our farm, sometimes I think about calling a cousin to see if they want to hunt here. Sometimes I think about going for a walk. Every time though, I think about going over to the neighbor's fence line, sitting on a post, and shooting warning shots up in the air for the deer that may be close to where one particular hunter is hanging out.

Life Quote: I'm never cooking again. ~ What I say when the giant turkey arrives, but honestly, we're pigs and it only lasts a short time.

SCOUT

On a farm, I have learned, you sometimes come across animals with "personality." We once had a white cow who was demented. She disliked everyone, but absolutely hated me. As soon as I came around, she huffed and snorted and pawed at the ground ready to squash me. I learned to scale fences like Spiderman that year. We've also had a pig who would rub against us like a cat, drop to the ground, and look up at us waiting for a belly rub, which I've now learned is quite common, but it was weird to me at the time. However, the most memorable of these personalities was a lamb named Scout. This animal had lots of personalities and absolutely no boundaries.

I am ashamed that I named this little monster after one of the most beloved characters in American literature, but at the time I was preparing to teach *To Kill A Mockingbird* to a bunch of tenth graders, and I wanted a funny introduction story about how much I loved the book. My sneaky and very intelligent husband came home one night asking if I could bottle feed a lamb whose mother wouldn't take him. That was the first warning, but I only saw a little tiny doll bottle followed by the cutest little lamb ever. You see, this was before I had a baby, so I had no idea that late night feedings were not a pleasant experience, no matter how cute the recipient.

"So, you'll take him," my husband asked slyly.

"Of course, of course, he's sooo cute!"

My husband made a mad dash out of the house because he was experienced in raising a bottle calf or lamb, knew the probable outcome, and didn't want to be around for the chaos and tears.

I volunteered happily, cuddling my new pet in my arms. I warmed up the first bottle as Scout ran from the living room carpet to the kitchen linoleum, pulling a Bambi on ice once he hit the hard surface, but repeating the process over and over until his bottle was ready. I checked it on my wrist as any loving mother would do. I burned the crap out of myself a couple of times, so this was good practice. Once Scout got the hang of feeding from the bottle, he'd chase me around the kitchen looking for it. I'd slump over with the bottle in front of his face and twirl in circles as he clickety-clacked around me. That stopped when I realized, as he was running in circles, his pellet poop was flying around my kitchen.

We kept him in a doghouse in the bathroom for about a week, then his constant crying through the night forced me to kick him out to a hutch in the backyard. I wasn't learning much about being a good mommy. I just wanted to sleep. As he became more comfortable outside, he became buddy-buddy with our dogs, Mops and Scooter, two little mutts who couldn't be considered farm dogs, more like lazy, sleepy dogs. Actually, yes, that is the definition of a farm dog.

Since they chased cars, so did Scout. He thought he was a dog. He would chase me out of the driveway every morning. I'd almost lose him, but then I had to open a gate, so he'd wait for me to get going again. I never ran over him, but he got a few serious bumps and never learned a lesson. Sometimes I'd have to call my husband when I reached the highway off our gravel road to tell him to call Scout back toward the house.

People would call us to say, "Ummm, I just saw your lamb out on the highway with a bunch of dogs."

It was really entertaining to watch people drive by the house, roll down their window to yell at the dogs chasing them, then stop for a "What the?" moment when they realized it was a lamb. Even the UPS and FedEx drivers recognized Scout as they frequently stopped by our house dropping off items which I ordered in an avoidance of going to a store. I'm making myself out to be pretty lazy, but I didn't want to put pants or makeup on, and when I'm at home I can just act like I'm not there when they drop off an item.

The first time they'd see Scout, I could tell they were thinking, "Wait, that's no poodle." They got use to him though and even offered Scout some dog treats.

Chasing cars was annoying, but he started crossing the line when he became overly aggressive. We never got down to business to castrate Scout like the other lambs, so a time came like any teenager, when Scout tried to fight or hump anything in sight. First, he tried humping my dog Mops. Mops became scarce after that, rarely making an appearance from the embarrassment of it all. Then, when I'd sit down on the ground, he'd try to headbutt me or hump me.

After that, it was anything and everything. Visitors, bushes, machinery, the porch stairs. We were only safe at the top of the stairs on the porch because Scout hadn't figured that out yet. When we'd want to leave the house, we'd try to sneak out slowly without making noise, and if Scout had noticed us before we made it to the car, we'd sprint, weave, and dodge him to get in our vehicles unscathed. When he finally figured out the steps, and we couldn't even get out the front door safely, we decided it was time to get rid of Scout.

It was time for my husband to take a bunch of the lambs to market anyway, so Scout had to go too. It was an ordeal getting him into the trailer, and when he was in there, he looked shocked. Since he was bottle fed, he was much smaller than the other lambs, and he was used to being much bigger than the other dogs.

Also, you could tell he was thinking, "There's some mistake. I'm a dog. Why am I in here with these awful, unkempt animals?"

My husband told me before I started taking care of Scout that I'd get to keep whatever he made at the sale. I haven't seen any of that money, of course, but it's payment enough to safely walk to my car. If somehow, he made it through the market without becoming mutton and he ended up on another farm, I just hope the best for that family, their cars, and their small dogs.

Life Quote: Sheep are supposed to be cute and cuddly, not disgusting predators. ~ A friend's now ex-husband after being terrorized by Scout. It might have been Scout's fault. We're still not sure.

Scout, the wonder dog!

CASTRATING PIGS

A common phrase that I've heard my husband mention ever since I've known him is this: "I waited too long and…" We missed a couple of opportunities because of this indecisiveness, such as farms or homes which we were thinking of buying when we were first married but in the long run those missed opportunities were for the best. Usually the wait is over something small that just creates a little more work. It's caused by the lack of hours in a day, but I still pick on his procrastination of certain chores.

One example would be "I waited too long and now I can't find the riding mower because the grass it too high."

Another example would be "I waited too long to feed you and now I'm in the doghouse because you're hangry."

That last one is a real dangerous situation, but one that I've really learned to hate is this: "I waited too long to cut the pig so I need your help because he's going to be a handful when I cut his nuts off."

It's not the technical language he used, but it's what I understood of it. Castrating a pig early is important for the flavor of the meat, but also for the strength of the marriage.

Letting an animal get a bit too big and dangerous to castrate is nothing new, so I'll give you a little background on the particular pig from this story:

- His name was Squealer.
- He was named after a pig in the novel *Animal Farm* by George Orwell. Remember, I was an English teacher.
- He had a sidekick who once filled our freezer, Napoleon, another character from *Animal Farm.* Napoleon was the head honcho, and the book is a representation of the Communist revolution. In the novel, he was a terrible leader, becoming fat and dictatorial after becoming too powerful, which reminded me of our Napoleon. He was fatter than Squealer and seemed to be in charge. Another reminder that I was an English teacher and am still a nerd.
- Squealer represented propaganda in the novel, in case you needed to know that for your Trivia Crack app. It's been on there. I've seen it. Remember, I was an English teacher, am still a nerd, and I like to spank people at trivia. If I don't win, I'll act like it never happened but carry a grudge for the rest of my life and try to demean you in other possible ways like Scrabble or Rock, Paper, Scissors.

Now that your literature lesson is over, I'll get back to the less artistic type of writing. Did you notice that last tidbit had nothing to do with the pig we had? I just tricked you into learning about classic literature. Don't be angry! You'll get your revenge by the end of this story...I get what I deserve.

Squealer was serving as our tiller for a while when our tiller broke, and he was doing a wonderful job, or that's at least what I thought at the time. The finished product was mentioned previously in the gardening section: hills, cockleburs, and a terrible looking garden. On the day he finished making a mockery of my garden, he was taken back to his own pen, held up by his hind legs, and castrated. It wasn't a punishment; it really had to be done.

When my husband suggested I help him, I didn't worry much. He didn't seem all that big to me. Like my husband had said, he waited too long, and this pig was big. The eyes can be deceiving, but after struggling with him and seeing his pighood thrown out on the ground, I can attest that he was a big pig. My quivering biceps could back me up on that one.

I didn't know the necessity of castrating pigs until I moved to the farm, so I'll explain why it's a must. Male pigs, a.k.a. boars, taste terrible if they are slaughtered and they've never been cut. I don't know the science behind this, but I've heard about how awful it is, and I think I'd be extremely upset if I bit into my BLT and it tasted rotten. That would be a waste of a perfectly good summer tomato.

So, on Squealer's big day (I feel like that would be an awesome children's book title, but a terrible story), my husband held him up so I was on one side of the fence and he was on the other. I held Squealer's legs so my husband could have both hands free. Of course, when I saw the blade coming down, I looked away. Usually it wouldn't bother me, but pregnant me, as I happened to be at the time, is a-whole-nother person (yeah, a-whole-*nother*...that means I'm serious and a little hillbillyish). Pregnant me complains a lot and pukes on a dime, so this was no picnic for my husband either.

As I was looking away, the pig started to live up to his name. He was squealing like a little pig, but he was more of a burly teenager, as I was quickly finding out. He started to wiggle and kick. My oldest son Aiden was holding his ears, playing nearby, then he got curious and wanted to know why we were hurting the piggy. Trying to explain to a three-year-old that you are helping the piggy, that you are trying to make the ham for next Christmas taste good, while your arms and lack of stomach muscles are burning from the position they were trying to keep, all while competing with your gag reflex, is a real challenge.

"It's...gulp...for...(swallow)...his own...(retch).... good!"

When I thought the whole ordeal should have been over, my husband started mumbling profanities, which meant Squealer was more attached to his nuts than we had originally prepared for. He was becoming increasingly squirmy, my arms were aching, and I wasn't feeling all that great. After what felt like an eternity, my husband was able to get one out. Then, before we could move on to the second, we literally scared the shit out of him, so I had to let go for a moment. Nausea! But I was able to control myself with a quick circle in the grass and a few deep breaths, then I took the hind legs back from my husband to finish the job. Of course, Squealer had just lost half of his pighood, so he was going to try and keep the other.

He started making quick kicks to throw me off, his squeals were nonstop, and they became deep. He was channeling his leader Napoleon, and the squeals seemed disturbing. My arms started shaking again. I was looking up at the clouds floating by. My son could have been running the chainsaw at this point, but I wouldn't have heard over the squeals and the gulping back of bile in my own throat.

My husband distracted me, as he said, "almost there." Then I heard it, as he was cutting, the tearing sound, and I started the dry heave body shakes.

At the eleventh hour of my convulsions, my husband finally yelled, "Got it!" and threw the one remaining nut across the field.

Simultaneously, my arms collapsed, and Squealer moved away quickly. Aiden was clapping at our success, and my husband was just repeating over and over, "Sorry, Sorry, Sorry!" to me as I tried to control myself.

Then it happened. Squealer turned on us, looked straight at me with no pity in his eyes, walked nonchalantly over to the last nut that was taken from him, sniffed, and licked it. I don't know what he did after that because it was all over for me. I was bent over in the grass with my three-year-old patting my back, saying, "Isss otay, Mommy," while my husband continued to repeat a more emphatic, "Sorry,

Sorry, Sorry!" but I'm pretty sure he was laughing too.

So, for those of you who are close family or friends, and receive a large ham or wonderfully delicious pork chops at Christmas time, remember the hard work and sacrifice that went into that pig. I lost two chocolate-covered, Casey's donuts that morning just so your dinner wouldn't taste like crap.

The next time we get a pig, I'll make sure I put a reminder on my smartphone instead of waiting for that dreaded conversation with my husband that starts with "Well, I waited too long again…"

Life Quote: Never wait too long after you've eaten Mexican food. ~ My husband's advice to our son about restroom etiquette.

RUDY

Every farm needs a good farm dog, and as long as I've known my husband's family, they've had more than a few farm dogs, but none were as good as Rudy. I'm not sure if Rudy was a good working dog, based on her routine in later life I'm assuming no, but she was pretty smart and super cute, so the rest doesn't matter. When I was first introduced to Rudy, she was an old dog but she'd hung on for a long time. Sadly, she passed away a couple of years ago, so this is dedicated to the dog, out of all the other farm dogs that have lived on this farm, and there've been a few, who had the most personality, or at least a personality that we enjoyed.

My husband picked up Rudy on a delivery route when his family still ran a dairy and delivered raw milk around the area. A lady on the route had a box of blue heeler-mix puppies. My husband's first thought was that blue heelers make good cow dogs and asked if she was giving them away.

She was.

He took one.

Did Rudy make a good cow dog?

No.

He never even heard her bark until she was three, but she was a good companion, loved to ride shotgun in the truck, and liked to be petted. I know personally that shotgun was her declared seat after she gave me the Rudy who-do-you-think-you-are look and wouldn't budge an inch when I tried to take her spot.

When John had Rudy spayed, she was the calmest dog at the veterinarian's office. When they pulled up to the office, she jumped out of the truck and just followed him, no leash required, while all the other animals were caged or leashed and fighting against it. Rudy walked out the same way, just a little slower. Quick note - this is no way to enter a veterinary clinic, so don't try this at home, but luckily for my husband, it didn't end in any terrible mishaps with a frightened cat or a little dog trying to prove a point because Rudy was chill.

After he had Rudy for two or three years, she was involved in an accident. My husband was out mowing pasture. Rudy was in the field chasing rabbits when she jumped out in front of the mower. My husband couldn't stop in time, and he knew he'd hit her, but she slipped into the woods quickly. He looked all over for her, and when he couldn't find her, he came back later with help. He even looked the next day, but no one could find her. They assumed that she had crawled away and died somewhere because she had to have had some major cuts, but after a few days, she showed up, lying next to a hay bale. She had a gash on each leg, just above the paws. One more inch and her paws might have been cut off. Her legs were already healing, so they took her home and let her rest.

The injury didn't slow her down. She healed and didn't show much sign of a problem, except when it was cold or rainy out. Then Rudy would scratch on the door and limp like she was hurt. As soon as you took pity on her and let her in, she'd go back to walking just like normal, curl up on the floor, and take a nap. She learned how to get what she wanted from that injury and knew how to work your emotions. Even after my husband moved out and lived down the road, if no one let her in at his parent's house, she'd come to our house and scratch on the door, hold up a paw, and we'd let her in.

That was a sure sign I'd be a sucker for a pouty face for the rest of my life.

Rudy also could work her magic to get a ride somewhere. As I said, shotgun was her seat and she'd show you a little teeth to say, "You're new around here so let's get this straight, this hair-covered side of the truck is and always will be mine."

It was entertaining to watch her sit upright in the passenger seat. If you hit the brakes, she'd raise a paw and steady herself on the dashboard. Sometimes she'd look over at you with a look like she was pitying *you* for being a bad driver. She'd sneak into any vehicle if she thought she'd get to go somewhere, but it did get her in trouble. The whole family had almost given her up for lost after they searched a week when she had gone missing. Someone just happened to open the door of an old car that no one drove anymore and out popped a very hungry and dehydrated Rudy. After that they were extra careful to check the vehicles for a napping Rudy before shutting its doors.

When Rudy was already pretty old, she accidentally ate some poison, or we guessed that's what was wrong with her. My mother-in-law called the local vet's office that evening, but they were already out on a call, so we ended up calling a vet in a neighboring county. I drove my Mustang, my husband and mother-in-law holding on to dear life, but I was speeding because I knew how much everyone loved this dog, and I just can't help but speed in any case, especially in panicked situations. Rudy lay in the back with a towel wrapped around her.

At the vet's office, things didn't start off great. He seemed very aggravated that he had to come in for an emergency call. After taking his time on the phone for what sounded like him returning messages from the answering machine while we patiently waited for him to check the EMERGENCY, he finally started examining her. He asked us indifferently, "What'd she eat?"

None of us were sure because none of us actually saw what it was; we just knew that she wasn't herself. Let me make this clear: IT WAS NOT OUR LOCAL VET! They would have *never* been so mean, as you'll see. The vet seemed angry because we didn't know and became extra rough with Rudy. It felt like a punishment because we didn't know what it was. The vet gave Rudy activated charcoal, which helped her vomit up anything that could have been poisonous in her stomach, then roughly pulled her off the table and said she'd stay the night.

As he complained about not knowing what she ate, he said, "She probably won't live because it may not be poison at all."

It was clearly a jab at us for not being able to give him more information.

We huddled together in the waiting room. None of us wanted to leave her there. We were all emotional and slightly traumatized, but he was seriously being mean, and if Rudy was going to die, we didn't want her to be alone. Against his advice, we took Rudy with us. Thankfully, after a rough night vomiting up some black charcoal and wobbling around like a drunk, she made a full recovery and gave us all a few more years to enjoy her.

In her older years, she was the dog in charge. She didn't bark much, but she'd growl at the younger, hyper dogs, and they'd leave her alone and chill out in her presence. Basically, she'd lay the smack down. To be clear, the other dogs were Pyrenees and Anatolian, much bigger than her, but they knew who was in charge as I did when I first tried to climb in the passenger seat of my husband's truck. She was still a sweetie though. She'd demand to be petted anytime someone was near but laid around most of the time.

After moving, we tried to lure Rudy over to our new home with treats and petting, but she always went back home to my in-law's house. I even dognapped her a couple of times when she thought we were just going for a truck ride as I was loading all our stuff from the old house to the new. It didn't work though because she'd get some dog food from our new house and trek it back through the woods to my in-laws. We didn't move far away (technically, I think we were closer to their house through the woods and not the gravel road) but I'm certain she would have found her way back either way. She was their pet and she liked her home, but she wasn't afraid to snag an extra meal here and there. When my boys are older, I hope they get a dog like Rudy. Even if she didn't turn out to be a good cow dog, she was one of the best pets you could ask for.

Life Quote: Heaven goes by favor. If it went by merit, you would stay out and your dog would go in. ~ Mark Twain

MOPS

We've had a lot of dogs out here on the farm. Some of these dogs are strays that just show up, sniffing out the bunnies and loose chickens. Some are drop offs from lazy people that no longer want to take care of their pets and randomly think, "Hey, they'll be taken care of if I just leave them in the middle of nowhere," which is actually true because there hasn't been a time we haven't fed and cared for random dogs that show up. They are always dogs that are super irritating so I guess I understand the need to flee from these dogs, but come on, I have enough irritation in my life.

Pierre, one that I named after reading a few French-set novels about Marie Antoinette, was one of those irritating dogs. I thought Pierre was a good human name for a dog because I pictured a human Pierre as someone who whined and moaned a lot, thinking that he was better than everyone, and would most certainly be uglier than everyone. My husband thought this wiener dog mix of something ugly was the greatest dog. I thought he was annoying. He disappeared. Maybe his owners missed him or he decided to go find the aristocratic family he was meant to be with, but I most certainly did not take him to a dog rescue in another city.

Some of these dogs we brought here as pets or as working farm dogs, and some dogs just appeared, out of nowhere, as little pups. Mops was my mystery dog. I already had Scooter, a little mutt, and I still have a sneaking suspicion that Mops was Scooter's pup, but Scooter wasn't very bright and I don't think she knew that. Probably why Pierre hit the road so urgently...puppy support is brutal!

I came home from work one day to hear a little squealing bark from under our house and when I took a peek, there was Mops trying to crawl out, but too little to pull himself out. I pulled him out and fell in love. He was a chubby little puppy, black and white, with a little brown. He didn't have a long nose like Scooter and I hadn't seen Scooter at the house for a couple of days. I'd seen her in the distance, but not at the house. I just assumed he was a drop-off that had found himself trapped, but as he got older he looked a little like Scooter and another dog that lived a mile away that I had noticed visiting a few months previous. Looks like Pierre was off the hook and I wouldn't need to call Maury to book a show with a dramatic DNA reveal. Beagles will travel a long way to get what they want.

My husband came home and found me playing with a puppy. Just what every husband loves to come home and find. He knew it wasn't worth the fight of deciding if this dog should stay or not.

Especially since I greeted him at the door with a puppy in his face and said, "Look, I found the love of my life."

Well, not exactly, but that's what he heard.

It had already been decided, as he clearly could tell as he looked around the room and saw a makeshift doggy bed, rags to wipe up any possible messes, and there were many, and the tiny lamb bottle from which I had been feeding Mops. I had named him already too, another name inspired by Marie Antoinette because her favorite dog was named Mops. I'm not creative, I just steal names from whatever

I'm reading about at the time.

He grew up to be my favorite dog of all, but he had all sorts of problems. Early on he became a cowering dog. He would ride with me to water my husband's calves every morning, and he got too close once, and they trampled and kicked him. He ran off and I couldn't find him all day. He finally found his way home and never seemed to enjoy farm life from that day on. We were kindred spirits in that way. Any time I helped in the corral, I was always the one to get chased for no reason at all, and I was going to hold a grudge with Mops. We were meant to be in Versailles enjoying French pastries!

He always held a fear of anything bigger than he was after that, even Scout, the bad lamb that I bottle fed, but that was completely understandable. Half the time Scout would run and play with Mops and the other half of the time he'd surprisingly ram his head against Mop's side, sending him yelping into the woods for protection.

Mops also suffered from an eating disorder.

Yes, I know this is something I shouldn't joke about, but I feel like it was true of my poor Mops. My poor little beagle mutt had an eating disorder brought on by bigger dogs pushing him around and then exacerbated by my husband's joy of picking on my sweet puppy. Early on, the bigger dogs would intimidate Mops, and he would wait until they had finished eating before he would eat. It wasn't like they would fight over food, but the chaos of having Scooter hogging it all (and Scout because he loved dog food more than the dogs) was just too much for Mops, and he'd hang back and get the last few nibbles. If another dog approached, he'd sit there quietly and wait until the other dog ate the rest or left him in peace.

I started feeding him a little extra later on when he'd hang around the house while the other dogs did the whole farm dog thing, like chase cows when they weren't supposed to, chase cars when they weren't supposed to, and lay around and let coyotes do their thing when they weren't supposed to.

I only exacerbated his problem by catering to his whims and he became more and more unlikely to eat in front of any animal, humans included. My husband is partly to blame for this because he quickly picked up on the hilarity that our dog was a weird eater and would purposely tell Mops he was fat as he'd sneak up to the house while Mops was finally alone, serenely eating his dog food. He ruined his peaceful moment and Mops would run off without finishing and I'd have to hope that Mops would come back during the night and finish his food.

It actually only happened a couple of times until my husband felt bad for picking on Mops, but Mops and I still gave him the evil eye when he'd come around during dinner time.

Not that Mops ever went hungry. I caught him plenty of times eating dead rabbits or moles, so maybe it wasn't that he was ashamed to eat in front of others because he was fat (as my husband claims). Maybe it was because he had the instincts of an ancient hunting dog and being fed dog food without the hunt shamed him. I'm going to stick with that to give my poor Mopsy a little dignity.

We had Mops for a long time. When we moved to our newly built construction zone not far away from the old house, he promptly took up residence without any complaint, unlike the cat, who never really settled down and took up residency in a neighbor's barn instead. That was probably more of a referendum on the incomplete construction of our new house than the fact that we moved. Cats are very persnickety and judgmental.

Mops would come into the house on a winter's night and he slept on a couch, actually his own couch. We called it Mops' couch. He was quiet all night long, never had an accident even though he'd never been a house dog before, and as soon as I'd wake up early in the morning before light, I'd see his bright eyes looking at me as I entered the kitchen. As soon as I'd turn on the light, he'd hop off like he'd been up for a while just quietly waiting for me and head for the door. He'd head outside, do his business, and I'd watch him heading down the hill in the direction of my in-law's farm, probably to hang with the other dogs for the rest of the day.

He was an all-around good dog, but sadly, he disappeared a while ago. I hope nothing terrible happened to him, and I'll just hope that he decided it was time to go out and become the ancient, self-sufficient warrior pup that he was always meant to be.

Life Quote: When a man's dog turns against him it is time for a wife to pack her trunk and go home to mama. ~ Mark Twain - Okay, I'll stop with the Twain quotes, but I'm from Missouri so I can't promise that I'll actually stop.

Safety First,
Or Last,
Or Forgotten

∞

A farm is a great place to raise kids, as people love to say, but it's ironically also a place to find a million ways to get hurt. My husband has fallen into a posthole he dug and then discarded and forgotten about. He hurt his ankle badly and I made him go to the doctor, so of course, now, I'm blamed for the $70 bill instead of blaming himself for leaving a large hole in which to fall. Also, come on - $70! That's a steal and it's including a brace he was charged for which he wouldn't even wear. I should be thanked for finding us insurance that only cost $70 for an emergency visit. Well, not an "emergency room" visit, but our local rural doctor who had a bit of time during her lunch break to see yet another posthole accident kind of "emergency." He should also go out and fill in the five other postholes that were also discarded and in which I have also fallen. Blessedly, I was descended from a long line of cankled German women, so I'm safe from catastrophes such as that.

My husband has also come home with smashed fingers, bloodied gashes, and hunched over in pain from backaches, but those are too many to count and would fill a book on their own. I think their frequency are picking up with old age, but we're not ready to admit that yet. Most of the time he's not willing to tell me how it happened anyway in fear that it would end up in a hilarious blog (my description, not his), and he keeps his own counsel and begs for a smashed-up Tylenol in some pudding which I will not do for him.

So, in all humility, this book is about my take on farm life, and this section is what I deem unsafe, or gross, or things that might cause me to lose my mind, and in turn, become unsafe. If my husband wants to, he can write his own safety book, which I assume won't be nearly as funny if I had written it. It would probably also focus on my many flaws, and no one wants to buy a book that's only a paragraph long, right?

∞

ELECTRIC FENCES

Even though you don't want it to happen, you try to pay attention so it doesn't happen, and you take extra precautions to prevent it, you are bound to get shocked by an electric fence if you live your life surrounded by cows. I've only been shocked full blast once in ten years and that was enough for me.

Back when my husband and I were still dating, and I was still glad to help him whenever I could, he convinced me to water his calves every day. It was at the farm we currently live on, but we hadn't built our house yet, so I would drive over, park at the end of the nonexistent driveway, and walk into the lot where the calves were. I'd fill up their water tank and sometimes feed them if they were bottle calves. This was July in Missouri, so I'd be hot, sweaty, and beet red from exertion even though I'd usually do this chore first thing in the morning. I also learned very quickly that little calves, left to their own devices, are kind of idiots. This chore generally included finding them, chasing them, and some serious basketball defensive moves to get them to go where they actually wanted to be but were too stupid to know it.

I've often thought I wasted so many hours at tortuous basketball practices in high school just trying and failing to be a mediocre player, but now I see that God had a plan for me to master a defensive slide good enough to stop a calf from escaping the corral. One really hot afternoon, so hot that I was watering the calves for a second time that day after an excruciatingly long battle leading the calves to water, my husband showed up on the tractor as I was going back to my car. He was going to brush hog and asked if I'd like to ride along. I was drained, it was so very hot, and I needed some water, but I went along anyway because love makes you do stupid things. If you've gotten a read on my husband yet from these stories, you should be picturing a tractor without a cab, therefore, no A.C. It was truly and honestly love because I was feet away from my wonderfully air-conditioned car as I climbed on the tractor. We rode along for I don't know how long. I was sweltering and was losing track of time. Dehydration was getting me down. Finally, we went back to my car, and that's when I realized my keys were missing.

If you learn anything about me while reading this book, you should by now know I'm the kind of person who loses keys frequently. That's just who I am. Take it or leave it.

Picture it. I reached into my pocket, finding nothing, knowing, remembering that they had been in my pocket when I took my initial walk out to the calves, then turning and looking out at what seemed like endless acres in which I had either run while chasing calves or rode through while on the tractor. It was summer time, the grass was tall and thick, and even in the places that had been cut, it was just so.... much.... area. It seemed hopeless, but my future husband who knew I'm the kind of person who loses my keys often and still married me anyway convinced me to look for them with him. I wanted to cry. I was lightheaded and cranky by this time, but I had no other choice. My other set of keys had been M.I.A. for a few weeks, lost at work, and wouldn't reappear for another six months.

Yes, I know there are organized people out there who are thinking, "What an idiot! I would not have gone one day without having two sets of keys. I bet she learned a lesson that day."

You would think so, but I'm currently down to one set of keys again, and I'm pretty sure it's been multiple years since I've seen the other set, and it's very likely that I lost them the day after I got my current car.

We looked and looked, did what every mom suggests, and retraced our steps with no luck. My husband's uncle Roy, who lives right next to the farm, noticed us and came out to ask what we were doing and suggested that he help with a metal detector. His uncle is the sweetest person, very helpful and quiet. I was sunburned, tired, and hot, so much so that I thought I was going to be sick, but I agreed because he wanted to be helpful, and I knew that if we left, he'd be out there anyway looking for them all night. We needed to help and give him a deadline of when to stop. Between his yard and the farm is a barbed wire fence with an electric wire three-quarters of the way up. Roy handed my husband the metal detector and started to climb through the wires as I held them apart while keeping my distance from the hot wire.

I was so hot, sweaty, and tired though. I kept my eyes on the hot wire, yet, while Roy was climbing through, I could see the wire getting closer and closer, but I couldn't stop my body.

I was mentally screaming, "Noooooo!" but my body was too tired to pull back.

As Roy was halfway through, the electricity popped on my shoulder. I don't know if it was from my exhaustion, or since I was holding metal, or the voltage was high, but it really, really, really hurt. It was ranked as the most painful experience of my life until I experienced childbirth. It felt like a very long time, but it was just a split second. As the current ran through my body, I let go of the barbed wire, leaving Roy trapped to listen to the cursing that flew from my mouth like a sailor.

"God d&#@, M$*)@% #*&@#$, @#%^& (# @%!& @)&^ #%^&@(%......." And on and on and on.

It went on quite a while.

When I finally looked back at Roy, still trapped under the barbed wire that I had let go of, all he said in an almost preacher/southern gentlemen way was, "Oh dear."

I never did find those keys and at that point I really didn't care. I'd rather leave my keys in the car with the windows rolled down and let it get stolen before I went through that mess again, but again, as I said before, I'm still wandering around living life on the edge with one set of keys. I'm a mom now. Let me be crazy in this one respect, okay. I've become extra vigilant about the fences though, keeping a healthy distance, and I generally talk my way out of farm chores anyway. My husband already married me. No need to impress him with helpfulness or shaved legs anymore, right?

Life Quote: The fence isn't hot, it's unplugged, I think...Maybe it's on, ah, no, I'm sure it's not. ~ What my husband says every time I ask him about a fence that I have to go through.

GOOD WEATHER

Once, while taking a wonderful hike, enjoying the warm weather, I was reminded of all the dangers (mostly made up in my own mind) that are lurking around during warm weather. I sun screened and bug sprayed us, dressed appropriately, put the baby in a front carrier, which I regretted later because he was a massive beast even at birth, and set off on the hike. We searched through the woods for morel mushrooms since it was a sunny day after a rain, and also because we're Missourians and that's what we do on a nice spring day.

The boys and I had no luck. Thankfully, my husband found some mushrooms later in an unnamed, undisclosed location. Seriously, I'd tell you, but even I don't know where he goes. I know the general direction, but I'm pretty sure he turns back around and ditches his trail so I won't know where he gets them. On this particular glorious day, we were just circling the woods near the house.

We'd been out for just 30 minutes, which was 30 minutes too long in my book, as my back was screaming out, "Put that chunker in a stroller next time!"

Then, suddenly, I screamed in pain, not from my back giving out, which was certainly going to happen soon, but from a sharp pain in the bottom of my foot.

I hopped to the nearest clear spot where I could basically lie down because remember, I have a baby in a front carrier and getting a good sitting position on the ground doesn't exactly work with a front carrier. After hopping around for a moment, I found a good spot to lay down as the baby drooled in my face, all while throwing my foot up over me so I could see what I had stepped on.

All the while, my oldest son stood over me and said as before, "It's otay, Mommy, it's otay."

He was getting older and could comfort without as much baby talk...and it was bittersweet.

I assumed that it was a thorn from a thorn tree, which are rampant around here, and I was correct. I had a battle with another thorn tree about five years prior, and it left me limping for weeks, my calf turned a few shades of red, then purple, and the doctor couldn't get the whole thing out because this particular species of thorn has tiny, microscopic thorns that hold them in place, and when you pull, the thorn just breaks apart. I was pregnant at the time of my first thorn experience and couldn't get an X-ray, so they just let it go, and it finally came out months later. I still have a gross scar from it.

I was expecting the worst when I was carefully peeling my shoe and sock off to inspect the thorn. It had broken off and was sticking out of my foot about an inch, which was a good sign for at least trying to remove it where I was. I knew there wasn't much I could do about it, so I quickly yanked the thorn straight out, and surprisingly, the whole thing came out. Yeah, it hurt, but not like before.

"It's otay, Mommy, it's otay," my son repeated again and again as I grimaced and tried not to say anything that he could repeat at school and end up in trouble.

As I inspected the thorn, I realized it was quite dry, so it had been off the tree for a while, less likely to be as potent as before. I put my shoe back on as the baby yanked a chunk of hair off my head, giggling at his wonderful luck to be nose to nose with Momma, just in enough range to pull hair, scratch at my eyes, and bite me, of which he was doing all three. My foot was bleeding, but didn't hurt bad, so I had been lucky.

I was done with this hike though, so I slowly got up off the ground with help from my four-year-old and limped back up the hill toward the house, dragging that four-year-old kicking and screaming after he realized that the hike was over.

When we finally got home, and I was able to get the little monster out of the carrier and take a good look at my foot, I found seed ticks crawling up my leg, so it was a mad dash to the shower for all of us. So much for bug spray. So much for a nice little relaxing hike. It then occurred to me that it was finally the time of year when we all want to spend the day outside, but outside is full of a mom's worst nightmare. Now, as I step outside, I think of the following:

1. Ticks, mosquitoes, bees, and other bugs - I use bug spray, but I think we've got some super bugs around here that also think my oldest has some sweet blood because he seems to be the one that gets the worst of it. We jokingly say it's because he's so sweet, but he is the one out there hugging trees, playing in the mud puddles, rolling in the grass, and collecting bugs, so he's just asking for it. At least when we come in, the other bugs are of no concern, but the ticks could be hiding anywhere and everywhere, so it's a continuous search. Currently, if you see my son scratching in an inappropriate area, it's because we didn't catch one in time.
2. Snakes - It's actually rare that I see one, but they're here, and they give me nightmares. In years past, I have found snakes hanging over our front door, curled up on the wood pile, and slithering across the lawn, so I know they are just waiting until I'm not expecting it. This summer, one was found

hanging out in the kitchen like he owned the place. I've never been the same. Recently, at the local park, I saw a snake jump out of the water and swallow a large frog whole as my oldest sat on the edge of the water and cheered in astonishment. The movie *Lonesome Dove* has ruined me, so I yelled at him with agitation to "Get away from the water before you get eaten!!!"

3. Thorn trees and poison ivy - As I said before, thorn trees are bad news bears. It hurt, really, really bad when I got stuck with one. I'd hate it if one of my boys got stuck with one. I'm constantly on the lookout when we hike around the farm in case there's a thorn tree up ahead. Poison ivy, not so much. I was not in Girl Scouts growing up so I didn't learn those helpful identifying marks of nature. Everything looks like poison ivy to me, so I've basically given up looking for that. Usually, I end up getting it off my husband's laundry anyway. I can always tell when he's walked through it or has gotten into it recently. My hands and arms get it from putting his jeans and shirts into the washer.
4. Sunburn - Babies over six months have their own sunscreen, older than two have the awesome spray kind so I can catch the boys at a run, and since the spray stuff gives me a rash, I've got my own sunscreen as well. It's a whole process before leaving the house, but we're all super pale too and need multiple layers throughout the day. By the evening, we're a layer of dirt and lotion mixture, so it looks like we have a tan, except for the one spot Mommy almost certainly forgets to cover. It never fails. When my oldest was a baby, we went out to the river and I sun screened him repeatedly, with thick layers, and then put a hat and sunglasses on him because I couldn't get the lotion near his eyes. Of course, the next day he looked like a red-eyed raccoon because he kept pulling the hat and glasses off and got sunburned in the only

place without sunscreen.

Planning for a summer hike in this area is like planning a vacation. It's kind of exhausting, and it's usually not worth the effort you put into it, but we all keep doing it. My boys are heathens and a heathen's natural habitat is in the sweltering heat of a Missouri summer. I'll continue to be on the lookout so I don't get stabbed with a thorn, pour on sunscreen and bug repellent, and sweat my behind off for a day of Vitamin D because it's Missouri, and Missouri has decided that March will be spring, April will be summer, and May will be fall. Expect snowfall by Memorial Day and then start the routine over in weeklong increments unless there's a drought. Now, that's just miserable. To make your life easier, take the first precaution against ticks, and shave your kid's head like I did. It shaves off about ten minutes of time from the inevitable tick-check that you spend, sitting like a bunch of monkeys in the living room, checking any hiding spots where a tick might be sucking all the sweet blood from my stinky, sweaty, and sweet little munchkins.

Life Quote: You need to check my butt crack. ~ My husband, every time he has to check himself for ticks.

WOOD STOVE INCINERATOR

Missouri weather has shown us time and time again that it has a mind of its own, and just when we think we don't need to fire up the wood stove, it drops below freezing in May for kicks and grins, mainly my kicks, and I have no idea who grins. We've also had winters when we've barely used the wood stove, but eventually and randomly it does get its fair use. I personally believe that if I have to put up with the nuisance of a wood stove, then I get to rule it the way I see fit. Dirtying myself with wood chips, hauling wood across the yard, smashing multiple fingers multiple times, and dealing with wood smoke, which leaves me hacking and gagging, are all wonderful reasons for me to build a giant fire and keep it at least 90 degrees in our house for the rest of the summer… oh, sorry, I meant winter.

This gives us the impression that it is summer, that the sun is out, and that seasonal affective disorder isn't doing some real damage to our psyches all winter long. I also have to be the overseer of all that ends up in the wood stove because wood is just a fraction of what my husband thinks is acceptable to burn.

There are a few things that I will throw in, things to layer the wood when I start a fire, like the never-ending cardboard packaging from Christmas presents, junk mail like the fifteen or so Dish Network or Direct TV flyers we get a week, credit card bills that I don't want my husband to see, and the overflow of coloring pages and crafts overtaking our refrigerator, after bed time obviously. Shredders are a waste of money in our house. A pile of old tax returns just increased the temperature in our house the other day by 4°.

There are also the imaginary things that we say are in the wood stove. When my oldest son is having a particularly rough day, and that's putting it nicely, we resort to just plain meanness to get him to straighten up. You'll find him sitting on the floor having a meltdown after we've informed him that since he threw a toy at us, we threw it in the wood stove. Actually, it's hidden in the kitchen cabinets, but when you've been backhanded by Buzz Lightyear, you can't really be patient, so the wood stove becomes a very harsh parenting tool. The toys show back up later when he's done something nice, and we just say that we found a new one since he was a good boy.

"This one has the same broken arm as my old one. I wish I would have gotten one that wasn't broken," he whines as my husband mumbles under him breath that maybe he should have thrown Buzz in the fire.

My husband also had a little party by the wood stove once when I made him go through all his files and he discovered that he still had a ton of paperwork from his time as an owner of a trailer court. He sat by the wood stove, put his feet up on another chair, threw in piece by piece as he plucked a few cans of Busch Light from a little cooler sitting next to him.

I'm pretty sure I heard him singing too… "This is my fight song, take back my life song" in a high soprano, no joke.

Rental property is a bitch!

He doesn't stop with the old papers and that's a big problem. I'm very sure that we are breathing in some really toxic fumes. One winter, when I was pregnant with the newest little monster in our house, I would open the bathroom window and take deep breaths when a chemical smell would take over the house from something my husband threw in the wood stove in fear that I would birth a two-headed monster.

What are these objects my husband deems safe for the wood stove which are sending carcinogens straight into our lungs? It's a wide variety of things, so I've completed yet another bullet style list for your musings:

1. A really stinky diaper that the Diaper Genie just can't handle. Diapers are generally indestructible, except in a massive 1000-degree wood stove.
2. Containers from the refrigerator that have been hidden behind larger objects for a year or two and now have developed into their own species of mold. He does the dishes most of the time, so I don't blame him. I take the high road and wash them, but only after opening them up outside, throwing the contents at the pigs, and running as fast as I can to remove myself from the perimeter of stank.
3. Any plastic packaging that doesn't have a recycling symbol on it, and when I haven't taken out the recycling and it begins to overflow, I'm pretty sure the recycling gets it too.
4. A mouse on a sticky trap. Blah! Thank goodness for the cat, so we don't have to deal with mice or the thought of my husband just chucking one into the fire. But yes, this has happened before.
5. Bale wrap. He has learned from experimentation that it starts a ridiculous fire that sounds like a train roaring through the wood stove but also puts out a nasty chemical smell - a.k.a. the first step in acquiring lung cancer. He creates a little pile of it next to the woodpile, just outside our door for those

pesky evenings when the green wood is the only thing left in the woodpile and we're all too tired to walk the extra 50 yards to get more from the massive woodpile by the garage.

7. Oil. That's right. You read correctly. Oil. He had some used oil that he started putting in there until the smell became even too much for him, but it sure did add a little oomph to the flame.

Please start that Go Fund Me account now to send my boys to college because between the fumes and the shear stress of living with three boys, I won't make it long. At least the fumes cover up any stinky boy smell which has invaded my house. Febreze does nothing for that. So far, only minor problems have developed from his experimentation with incinerating things, which he says would be cured if I would just take anger management classes.

Life Quote: You need to take a vitamin. ~ My husband, which is code for "taking a chill pill or something stronger," which he learned from my dad when he said it to me once when I was angry.

PUMPKIN PIE

My husband once mentioned that a pumpkin or watermelon was growing down the hill from our house, not anywhere near our garden. "Hmmmmm...that's cool," I thought, and then forgot all about it because my domain is the house and the 20 yards around it. I wasn't interested because it was farther than my concern.

John's not a gardener, so he couldn't tell what it was until it started to take shape, and then, like a stroke of autumn magic, it took the shape of a pumpkin. Honestly, I didn't believe him because I just thought it was some random plant overtaking the hillside like most of the cockleburs, thistles, and other various weeds overtaking the boundaries of our yard. I also didn't want to take the short walk to go look because that would be followed by trudging back up the hill and that seems suspiciously similar to exercise. He mentioned it again, and again, until I finally took a look.

How cool, huh? Just a random pumpkin popping out of nowhere. Not really nowhere, a very important *where* actually.

It was growing just off the lagoon.

For all the city people that think of a lagoon as just a small body of water, I must inform you that a lagoon in the country is, um, well, it's where the poop goes.

We aren't hooked up to sewer lines out in the boonies, so our options are to have a septic tank or a lagoon.

It's down the hill from our house near the wood line. Technically, it's a little way off, but the vine had grown up the hill from the lagoon, creating a giant pumpkin. I thought vines would naturally grow in the easiest direction - downhill, or up the fence - but no, it had chosen the steep hill, trying to make its way toward our home. Of course, it was giant! It had been fertilized once a day by most of us and anytime my husband wants to sit down and read a book in the bathroom. I'm taking a big leap here, but I'm sure it's just once from my husband too because I know he's just sitting in the bathroom enjoying quiet time any other time he hides in there during the day.

My first question was where did the pumpkin seed come from that started this massive vine? In the past we have thrown the old pumpkins in the garden, with my intention every year to begin a compost pile, which never happens. When we have pigs, we will give them the pumpkins, which they love, but the garden and the pigs were on the other side of the house. The only other thing I could think of was the one time I have baked pumpkin seeds with my son.

He saw it on television and then again at the library when the librarian read a story about carving a pumpkin, and they briefly mentioned saving the seeds for a snack in the story. He doesn't miss a thing, so we had to go directly home, carve a pumpkin that I never had the chance to carve at Halloween. It was just then coincidentally serving as our Thanksgiving decoration, so we baked the seeds just as the recipe on the back of the book described, with a little season salt, butter, and my secret ingredient/technique. It wasn't that difficult of course, consisting of some prep work, ingredients, and a baking sheet, but I'm not a baker, so after five minutes too long, I could smell burning pumpkin seeds as we built a Lego castle in the next room.

My secret technique? Burning - I burn everything.

That did not deter my then three-year-old. He wanted some pumpkin seeds and he ate quite a few. The rest ended up in the trash. One seed must have survived the burning ritual I call cooking, and therefore, I'm concerned that one seed somehow kept its whole shape through the digestive system and survived the monsoon through the plumbing. The pumpkin must have come from poop and was fertilized with poop.

I wanted nothing to do with this disgusting poop pumpkin.

Obviously, other scenarios are probably more accurate, like a bird picking up a seed from the compost pile and dropping it on its way back to its nest in the woods. It may even have been from a Halloween pumpkin from the previous year that went astray. I buy A LOT of Halloween pumpkins. It wouldn't be shocking to know that when my son was so deliberately moving them from their designated spot to new spots all over the yard, one rolled down the hill.

But I couldn't shake the feeling that it was a poop pumpkin. I decided that it would stay in its spot where it would eventually rot.

I kept an eye on it though. It was pretty large, better than anything I've ever planted. I was a bit jealous because I had now found the secret ingredient to make my plants flourish but there was no way in hell that I would ever use my new knowledge. Soul crushing!

As the days went on though, I realized it would never turn completely orange. It stayed a green shade with some orange stripes, as it did continue to grow, but the sheep were moved into the field behind our house and started eating it. They nibbled the outer layer off, then it froze and thawed, froze and thawed, cracked, smashed, and entered the circle of life as it slowly disintegrated into the soil.

I spent the rest of that Thanksgiving season, doing exactly what you'd expect from me. I'd harass my family and friends, trying to convince them that I had made the pumpkin pie on their dinner table from the poop pumpkin. That's what Thanksgiving is all about, giving thanks for those people in your inner circle who have a good sense of humor while scooping up a slice and asking for some Cool Whip, and giving thanks for the jokes that reveal who in that inner circle doesn't trust you at all.

Life Quote: I know you didn't make this pumpkin pie because it's not burnt. ~ Everyone that I tried to fool.

TORNADO SEASON IN MISSOURI

It's tornado season, and if you're reading this in December and this statement seems to be true for you, you must live in Missouri. I feel like that is becoming more and more true the older I get, so I just consider it a possibility at any time in Missouri because our lovely weather patterns jump from a warm, 82-degree Tuesday straight into a snow drift on Wednesday. When the topic of tornados comes up, in December or April, I always feel it is my duty to be the mom, tell everyone to be safe, listen to warnings, and get to a basement, even though, if you are once like the younger me, you don't take that seriously until you're hauling ass into the basement seconds before the tornado takes the house above your head.

If I told you this whole story, it would be a book on its own with a different version from each family member involved, and it would be told in completely different tones, from my father-in-law's low key attitude that it could have been worse, to my more exaggerated take that God was sending his wrath down on me as punishment for using his name in vain every single time I would stub my toe on our awkwardly positioned coffee table (but I still do that so I learned nothing). That's too much to get into, so I'll give you the beginning - just two idiots trying to figure out if it was serious enough to take cover - and you can buy the whole book later.

Before my husband and I built our house, we lived in a trailer on his parent's farm, so number one, we were asking for trouble living in a trailer because tornadoes hunt them down and eat them for breakfast. Number two, we only went to his parents for food, so it was awkward to go down for shelter.

There had been tornado warnings all day. In fact, earlier in the day, I had been at my mom's house 20 miles away, looking out the front door for a pending tornado. As rain poured down, the sky turned green, trash cans flew down the street, and a neighbor's obnoxious ten-foot fence toppled into the side of their house.

My mother screamed from the basement, "Get down here before you get sucked out the front door!"

She also kept calling my cellphone too after deciding she wasn't going to risk her life by coming back upstairs, ranting that I was going to be killed, but I waited out the storm and the tornado fizzled out a couple miles away. Thinking I was safe for another tornado season, I drove home.

The rest of the afternoon had bouts of quiet, rain, lightning, wind, and hail that my husband continued to work through. The work never ends on a farm. He came in later, showered, and we were continually interrupted in our T.V. watching by updates that we didn't care about and phone calls from his mother pleading with us to come down to their house to hang out in the basement. There wasn't a T.V. in that basement. We weren't budging.

Then, as we were getting super-pissed about the tenth interruption during our favorite television show, we noticed the wind pick up as the underpinning on the trailer rattled incessantly. Again, we were in a trailer! We were just asking for it. Our dog was howling and really wanted out of the house. Then the meteorologist started naming towns that we knew. Not the normal towns that still have a post office, but towns that had a heyday in the 1800's and were now only gravel road names. If you know the names to places like Steinmetz, Pumpkin Center, and Bunker Hill, it means it's time to go to the basement, not make the last-minute decision to drive to the nearest basement. The projected path of destruction within the next five minutes was right at us.

And this is what we had been left with, yet we stalled.

First, there was just panic to stall us, running around like chickens with their heads cut off.

Then, we started asking each other the question, "What do we take?"

It was already in our heads that we'd come back to nothing. It was a trailer, remember. That tornado was like UPS and had our address - delivery was guaranteed. I grabbed my cell phone and my bra (since we were guests), and my husband grabbed nothing. We obviously wasted some time looking for expensive items we should save. It quickly dawned on us that we didn't have any.

Last, it was the dog causing us to dawdle. As soon as we opened the door, my dog Scooter shot out and disappeared. We called for her for a while but gave up when the wind started shifting. We didn't realize at the time that we had not abandoned her for safety; she was abandoning the idiots that had trapped her in the house for so long. Animals are smarter than we are.

After a very quick drive down the road, we made it to my in-law's basement, literally seconds before the tornado barreled over top of us. So much for debating whether to shut the front door when we ran in. It was no longer there afterward. The lesson here is simple: Hang out in the basement if you see one sign of a funny looking cloud. Well, that's what we took from it. For real, be safe and listen to your meteorologist or weather radio or mother-in-law. Life is too short for those shenanigans. Literally, it will flash before your eyes, all the sex, drugs, and rock-n-roll, the memories you can soberly remember, and you won't remember the reality show that you were stalling for.

Life Quote: Hail, Mary, full of grace, the Lord is with Thee ~ My mother-in-law reciting the Hail Mary over and over and over again as we piled up in the potato pit in the basement as pipes burst over us. She hasn't been to a Catholic church since she was in 4th grade but the Catholic came out in her that night.

CLIFFHANGER

I know, I can't just leave the story at that. First of all, we made it out okay. My father-in-law, who also was unwilling to miss a beat on his milk route and tested how long he could stay on route before the tornado hit, pulled up right behind us when we reached the house, so I didn't feel so bad that we waited until the last second. He was the silly one who sat outside the potato pit as the basement windows were shattering and water was pouring down over us from the pipes above (I still pray that it was only water). He watched intently as lightning crashed and glass flew around him and listened as he heard the boards above him start to crack and buckle under the intense pressure.

I often wonder if he was just in shock, knowing that all he worked for hung outside in the balance, or was he so at peace with his life that he thought, "Well, this is it, I kind of want to keep my eyes open for this."

I had my eyes tightly closed and was also reciting the Hail Mary with a few F-bombs in between for good measure so God would understand exactly how serious I was about all this.

When the freight train above us finally subsided, we slowly worked our way up the steps to the kitchen, but it was a struggle to get the door open. The stove had been pushed in front of the door. Once we finally got the door open enough to squeeze through, my mother-in-law started to cry. It was terrible to sit there and witness it. Her home where she had raised her three boys was gone. We were standing in the middle of the house, but to the right some unsteady walls were still there and to our left and above us was completely open. You could see lightning shooting across the sky.

I was in shock and my husband hugged me immediately, you know, one of those moments when you really know that your spouse loves you after you both could have died. It was a hug that said, "Oh thank God, we're alive, you're alive, I will live to see another meal that I won't help with at all. Thank you, Lord Baby Jesus!"

It was a struggle getting out of there. This wasn't the middle of town. It was right in the middle of nowhere. The fire department did start the rounds along the county roads, but somehow missed us, so we spent the next couple of hours finding a vehicle that wasn't upside down or in a tree. Thankfully, since my father-in-law owned a delivery dairy, we had plenty of white stalker vans to choose from and joyously were able to get one started (after a few tries but that was normal). Then we had to hunt down a chainsaw because trees had fallen over in the driveway, preventing us from leaving. The driveway looks like it leads to a deserted haunted house anyway, so I assume the fire department thought that surely no one lived down there. The five-foot potholes and washouts are deceiving on a normal day.

We made it out though, cold, wet, and tired, and definitely shell-shocked. As we drove down the gravel, deciding we needed to go to my father-in-law's parent's house in the closest town to let them know we were okay, we had to drive by our house. The windows were foggy but trees weren't down on the gravel so I was hoping that nothing had happened to my house, the little trailer about which I always complained, and which held all my worthless belongings inside. And yes, a little part of me was praying that my car went unscathed. It was a 2004 Mustang, the one and only new vehicle I will ever purchase.

Oh yeah, my dog too, I wanted to make sure my dog was okay. Listen, I was a little dazed by the whole thing. I may have forgotten about the dog.

As we came around the corner that was adjacent to our driveway, my father-in-law shouted out in his first real outburst of the evening, "It's gone! Your trailer is g-"

I let out a groan. "Uuuuuuuggggghhhhh!"

"Nevermind, it's okay."

"Wait, what?!" I climbed up closer to a window. Remember, we were in the milk van and I had been perched on a milk crate as we drove down the gravel. I mean, come on, I had already defied death once that night. He wasn't going to get me.

As I wiped the condensation and dust from the window, I could see our trailer, and my car, and they were perfectly fine. We pulled in the drive to assess the damage.

Other than the two bottle calves my husband had next to the house, which were whining in shock because their hutches had blown apart and away, nothing was amiss.

"Whew!" I said, but then I immediately felt like a jerkface because my mother-in-law was sitting right there, probably still listing all the irreplaceable items in her head which she had just lost while I was celebrating that my twenty something, childless belongings were all intact.

We decided to grab a couple of things for all of us to clean up with and headed to the grandparent's house to see if they had electricity and to let them know we were okay. We hadn't been able to use our cell phones during the whole mess, so it was the first time we were able to use the phone. Once we got there, I called my mom first and, for the first time, cried like a baby.

After cleaning up, we decided to go home, and we spent the rest of the night in fitful attempts at sleep. It was a surreal experience, and I now have the opposite spectrum of tornado safety (or any bad weather). I haul ass to the basement at a tornado warning, and even if it's just windy without any warnings, you might even catch me piling pillows and blankets in the corner, under a table, with an emergency box and some snacks.

I really think a snack during that long ordeal would have made the experience so much better.

The real lesson from this whole ordeal was how kind people are. When word got around that the house and dairy had been destroyed in a tornado, my father-in-law's customers, neighbors, and quite honestly, almost the whole county, just started showing up with food, supplies, and helping hands. They organized a clean-up day and everyone helped pick up debris, move vehicles and trailers with heavy equipment, and they even walked around picking up massive amounts of quarters that my father-in-law threw in milk jugs throughout the house. Where the old house was would be a metal detector's dream.

They now live in a beautiful timber frame home. They no longer run the dairy, but it was a good time to take it as a sign to slow down, so instead, my father-in-law ran for public office and my mother-in-law bought, in what I can only describe as, a shit-ton of goats.

It can't be described as a blessing in disguise because my mother-in-law would most certainly want her most precious possessions back. She received a painting from her artistic sister-in-law depicting a scene from inside the old house, as you can just see her boys playing in the yard through a window and it brought on waves of tears. Although it was a hard loss, losing a lifetime of work on the dairy, a home where your children were raised, and naturally their peace of mind, it did send them in a new direction and sometimes that's pretty cool too.

That tornado sent my life in a new direction as well. My husband and I had been looking for a farm to buy ourselves for quite a while before the tornado, and everything in our price range was snatched up before we'd even known it was for sale. We might have given up. We might have continued on, found a farm with a beautiful, completed home but with half the acres. Instead we bought half of my in-law's farm since they wouldn't be running the dairy cows, built (still building, technically) our own home, and have started raising our family within hiking distance of Grandma's cookies. It's oh, so stressful at times, and I question our decisions a lot, but the alternative is probably still stressful but without the many memories. I would probably not have been able to stay at home with my children, and not had the time to tell my stories. Their loss was our gain, and I hope they know how grateful we are.

Life Quote: Clouds in the sky, don't die. ~ My new paranoid 180 degree turn on my philosophy about the weather.

Home sweet home.

Last,
But Certainly Not Least,
Love

∞

I don't want to finish up this book and leave you with the impression that I absolutely hate farm life. I only hate it 49% of the time on Monday, Wednesday, Friday, and Sunday and 51% of the time the rest of the week. I only kid, I do love it, but I'm not going to 100% embrace it because that would leave me wide open to continuous requests to help more around the farm. In this last section of the book, I will sum up with a few things that I absolutely love about the farm because these are the things that get me through, that keep me sane on days when I want to move to town, go for a walk on a sidewalk, and not feel like I'm planning and packing for a vacation just to run errands that city folk do on a walk around the block. I have to remind myself that I'm lucky: I'm surrounded by greenery, I can see the stars and enjoy the quiet, and I can yell at my kids and the neighbors won't hear me.

∞

THE ONE OLD SCHOOL FARM WIFE CHORE THAT DOESN'T MAKE ME ANGRY (MOST OF THE TIME)

Hanging out clothes is not really just a farm thing. Everybody should have a clothesline. It saves money, and what's better than that? Some people don't like hanging their clothes out in town for everyone to see, but my Aunt Marcia has been hanging out her underwear near downtown Columbia, Missouri, for the last 32 years, and she's one of the smartest and most confident people I know, so everybody should follow this trend. In town, a clothesline is a choice, but on a farm it's an absolute must. Yeah, we like to save money in every possible way, but we also have numerous occasions when power washing poo-covered clothes from the line is a necessity.

I do not like these occasions. They are gross, and they just suck. I do, however, love, love, love hanging out clothes from a normal load of laundry. I said normal, but a lot of the time it's not normal, but I'll take all loads of laundry. I would even consider it as a second career if anyone would like me to do their laundry. It's a completely over-the-top obsession, and it's the best feeling ever. Hanging out clothes is my favorite thing in the world (except my sons, my husband, and pickles).

The reason it's the greatest is the sense of order it brings to my life, an order that can almost balance out the endless construction, animals in my yard, and little boys with slugs in their pockets. Although my life is completely unorganized, laundry is something I can organize quickly and beautifully. Yes, beautifully. Well, until I find a slug in a pocket, then it's just gross. When I say beautifully, I mean symmetrically. Nothing is better than something symmetrical and I can get that when I hang out clothes.

I work with this in mind: heavy clothes on the outsides of the line, light clothes on the inside. This probably sounds a little nutty, but other people have way more serious problems than a bit of symmetry OCD so let's not judge.

A really good clothesline, if I were the judge of some weird laundry reality show, is one with jeans on each side, t-shirts next, and underwear and socks toward the middle. It's a work of art, and it's relaxing until folding time. Reality shows have hit a peak and are coming up with crazy ideas to keep cashing in while they can, so maybe I should pitch this idea. I actually love to fold too, making perfect little pyramid piles, but when you have to do that later in the day when a three-year-old is awake, it gets a little hairy. He wants to snuggle in the sun-warmed clothes, unfold everything, knock over my pyramids, and use the laundry baskets as a ship. If I can get ten minutes to myself with an audiobook, folding clothes is a joy. Nothing is better than listening to Chelsea Handler say something so completely inappropriate that I couldn't even repeat it to my own mother to help me feel my own life is a little more under control.

Another joy about laundry and hanging out clothes is just being outside. I don't just do this routine during the summer. If the clothes aren't going to freeze in the upside-down hanging shape, I will hang the clothes out. Yeah, they'll still need some time in the dryer, but I got my time in the quiet outdoors at 6:00 A.M. all by myself. For someone who spends a lot of time cleaning a dark basement house, a little vitamin D goes a long way. I might be hanging out clothes in a snowsuit, but it gets done, except during any hunting season because I'm afraid I'll get shot.

The only downfall of hanging clothes out on the line would be the bees and wasps which like to hang around a clothesline. I really hope no one watches me get clothes down on a warm afternoon because it's a continuous dance with the bees. Between every line, my arms are flailing and a few times I've doubled over swatting at my head after thinking one had made it into the messy bun I call a daily hairdo, but it's usually a grasshopper. Actually, even after all these battles, I've never been stung at the clothesline.

My husband has been stung as a result of the clothesline though. I've witnessed one of those "It's not funny, but it's kinda funny" moments as my husband has danced out of his pants after shockingly discovering a bee made its way inside his pants and lay in wait for him to get them up. It really wasn't funny (but it kind of was). I'm a bad person!

I know, I have problems. The bee in the pants is not one; you all know you would have laughed. My obsession with laundry might be the problem. Needing symmetry on the clothesline to get a bit of relaxation out of my day is weird. Creating pyramid piles out of the clean clothes is a waste of time, but I'm going to keep doing it. No judging because some of you run marathons and ride horses and teach Sunday school, all hobbies that I just can't fathom. Leave me to my laundry time! After all, after more than ten years together, I've just gotten my husband to fold towels the right way. That is a major accomplishment from his haphazard laundry technique of the past. It took years of training, and I'll be damned if we take a step back now. I'm already in the middle of training him on dishes with at least five more years to go.

Life Quote: I was just trying to help! ~ What my husband says, and what no micromanaging wife wants to hear, when he purposely comes out to help me hang out clothes, throwing them haphazardly over the line in no particular, freaking ORDER*!*

MY SWEET, MONSTROUS CHILDREN

Although I can complain 'til the sun comes up about farm life, I couldn't imagine raising my children in any other place. Whether they got it from the open spaces, or the open spaces just provided the urge, I am raising two explorers, curious in whatever crosses their path or whatever they hunt down. They dig in the dirt, play in the mud, and create a massive amount of laundry and stress, but it's so fantastic to watch them play.

They are both totally immersed in farm life. The oldest loves animals, loves the gross stuff, and has no fear of any large or small animal. The youngest loves animals, loves the gross stuff, but wants nothing to do with large or small animals if they are up close and personal, but he's warming up to them since he's already decided he'll be a farmer when he grows up. Just watching them in the corral is an entertaining experience. One picks up a lamb and chases the other with it, and as soon as we leave, the youngest cries because he didn't pet the lamb when he had a chance.

I've watched as the oldest has tipped over a plastic hay feeder, so it looks as if he's standing in a rat wheel, and then I watched as the youngest ran at it full speed to roll it away. Thank goodness he was too little at the time to create any speed to cause it to roll out of control. They were in an enclosed corral or I would have had to chase my oldest down a very long hill because, being the little dare devil that he is, he wouldn't have let go for the world.

They know disturbingly gross things about the circle of life farm-style and like to tell stories about an exploding placenta from a rotten sheep, cows which become carrion for the vultures after a particular nasty year of respiratory problems, and blood and bones and poop, and I'm supposed to seem interested in these topics and not grossed out or disturbed, but that's what makes it so wonderful. They learn things about life that other kids don't, they get to explore any time they want, and they have the space to grow and play that others don't.

It's a lucky life for two little precocious boys, and I love the life they get to live just as much as I love them.

If you're wondering, "Wait! Where are all the stories about the kids? She hardly mentioned them before," you are exactly right.

No, I'm not trying to respect their privacy at all. In this day of social media, I'm trying to ruin any chances that they can become president, which they'll thank me for later. I post too many pictures of them in spite of all the mommy articles which I've read explaining that I shouldn't do that at all. I can't help it.

Let's be honest, the basis for our profound love of social media is because it makes us feel special. More likes - I'm special! More comments - I'm more special! Lots of likes and lots of comments - well, it's obvious that my kid is cuter than yours. So, of course, I have a lot of stories about my kids, which some of you may have seen in my blog. The reason I have not included many stories about my kids is because they are more numerous than the farm stories, so I've taken them all out in case this is successful and I can push another book onto you in the future.

Oh, sorry, this is supposed to be about how much I love my kids and the fact that they are being raised on a farm, not how much money I want to make off of them. As I've already said, the youngest wants to be a farmer, so I really need to get what I can right now so I can afford a decent nursing home later in life.

As I tell them all the time, I love them to the Saturn and back. Grandma tells them she loves them to the farm and back, but I'm not allowed to use that one because "that's Grandma's, not yours." We eventually just fight over other planets and galaxies until one of my sons says "I wuv you to emfimity (infinity) and beyond" in his best Buzz Lightyear voice and that is the greatest thing on Earth.

Life Quote: They get this from you. ~ Says my husband when our boys are being gross, are especially rowdy, or are just getting on his nerves.

OH YEAH, AND THAT GUY WHO LIVES HERE TOO

It is no secret in our house or to anyone who knows me that I lost my heart when I had my boys. They snatched it up, waved their treasure in Daddy's face and said, "So long sucker!"

It's been that way ever since. My poor husband has gotten the short end of the stick since February of 2012 (boy #1) and got negative of any stick in July of 2015 (boy #2). If we had another child, we'd probably get a divorce. Actually, I know we would because he thinks it would be better on our taxes if we were divorced and I could claim the single parent child tax credit. He really knows every possible way to save some money.

Here's my attempt to write a love letter to my husband so he knows that I'm here on this farm and on our worldly travels with him for the rest of my days (or until he leaves me in some castle in Europe because he's just plain tired of it). No matter what life throws at us, even on the farm in which I continually joke about, we'll face it together (but if he wants to buy a farm in Ireland, I'd definitely be down for that).

On our wedding day, one of the readings was from 1 Corinthians, the old wedding standby that I was okay with because it didn't say anything about me having to be obedient. I hate that word... obedient...barf.

Since the Bible doesn't have a copyright that I'll infringe on, I can quote it without getting in trouble. I'm not just going to quote it though; I'm going to quote and analyze like any mediocre English teacher on how well I've done on the passage as a married woman of ten years. Honestly, it's not all that great, but at least I can admit my flaws. Never in person though. In the middle of an argument, I will never admit when I'm wrong. I will be sitting in my ship, swearing it doesn't leak, as I sink beneath the waves, but I'm hoping my husband likes me enough to throw me a life preserver and never mention it again.

1 Corinthians 13:4-7 (not 8 because that one's confusing)

"Love is patient,"

- It's patient most of the time, unless it's a morning when I've gotten up early to make sure everything is ready for school, breakfast is made, and you sleep late to roll out of bed at 7:15 and ask if you can help me. Nope, I have no patience for that. I am also not patient when you drive, or when you do the dishes while I'm in the middle of making dinner, taking up precious space at the kitchen counter. I'm also not patient when we have to make a construction/design decision because I really have no idea how it should be either and you're asking a question that clearly shows I have no idea. Okay, so I said most of the time, maybe I meant half of the time. At least I can say I'm getting better, right? Maybe. I am patient when I rarely help with the farm so that's a plus. Just keep giving me tasks that I have no clue how to do and

I'll be a patient little helper.

"love is kind."

- I guess I could write more blogs about how great you are, but then I'm not sure I could make it funny. I am very kind for about three days out of the month, but that might just be hormones or when it's sunny outside. I'll work on not being so snappy for the rest of the month. In my defense, these are the things I do for you as an act of kindness: buy large quantities of tortilla chips, use all my precious homegrown tomatoes for your salsa, listen really hard when you talk about the stock market (over my head, but I listen), and cook some kind of potato instead of just having a salad. I guess that's not really much, but three out of four deal with food so I'm keeping you alive.

"It does not envy,"

- Oh, but it does envy. I envy the amount of uninterrupted sleep you get, the sheer lack of shame you feel about saying something inappropriate to people you barely know, the amount of money you have in the bank compared to me, the lack of parenting guilt you feel when you let the boys watch television when they're getting out of hand, and the lack of guilt you feel when you choose *Family Guy* over *Mr. Roger's Neighborhood* like I would have chosen. I'll work on the envy if you choose Mr. Rogers next time (or just hand me a wad of cash).

"it does not boast,"

- I'm sorry for the numerous times I have overly boasted for weeks on end after beating you in Scrabble and/or pool. I do very much love to do something I'm good at and then rubbing it in your face in the aftermath of a lashing. See, I just can't help myself. I'm also sorry for instigating competitions in a little bit of everything like racing our cars down the driveway when we happen to pull in near the same time or who can stack the tallest tower out of our children's blocks when we "clean up" while watching our Sunday morning church program called *This Week* with George Stephanopolous. We do go to church, just in the evenings, or at least I go most of the time. You say you haven't sinned enough to go on a weekly basis. Anyway, I'll try to schedule some time to play chess so you can beat me as much as you want, well, until I learn how to play well, and then I'll ruin that game for you with a quick vengeance and my superior intellect. Geez, I'm sorry, I just can't help myself. I'll let you win, that's all I can offer.

"it is not proud."

- I'm never too proud to say I'm sorry for standing in the way in our tiny basement dwelling, and never too proud to say sorry when I am not ready with dinner and have yet another meeting to go to, leaving you with the kids for the third night in a row. A volunteer's job is never done. But I am too proud to say I'm sorry when I argue with you over little things that irritate me, so I'll say sorry now, a thousand times over, for the thousand times in the next year that I will argue with you over those little, bitty, drive me up the wall, maddening things. I can't even list them now. They come and go and are never the same from day to day.

"It does not dishonor others,"

- Neither one of us came into this with much honor or prestige, so I think this is a moot point. And if this is a fancy way of saying love doesn't make fun of others, well, 200 pages in and I'm shit up a creek. You make fun of me just as much though, so we're even.

"it is not self-seeking,"

- I didn't marry you for your money (you never spend any) and you didn't marry me for my money (because you realized quickly, that the opposite of what you thought, I didn't have any). I will apologize now for starting the blog that led to this book, especially if I make any money off of it, because the whole purpose of writing a humorous blog was to either make myself feel better and/or to make millions off the sales and marketing aspects of it. It's definitely beneficial, mentally or monetarily. If it makes you feel any better, if it ever happens that I make millions, I'll buy you a tractor with a cab and pay for some counseling (for myself or you – you choose).

"it is not easily angered,"

- This is the only place I'm going to admit this, so enjoy it now, but I have a quick fuse and I have passed it down to my children. I will do my best to take a deep breath and count to four as Daniel Tiger has explained to the boys and they have explained to me.

"it keeps no record of wrongs."

- I do not currently keep a record of your wrongs, but check with me the next time I'm mad. I bet after it festers for a while, I'll have a few things to say, so sorry about that too.

There was a lot more to that reading, but the rest gets a little confusing and I'm already feeling a little raw from admitting all my faults. Oh, I've forgotten a few? Make a list and you can include them in your rebuttal book: *Desperate Farmers: Where's My Dinner?*

Okay, so now that I've made clear that if this were a graded course, I would receive a D- from a very generous teacher, and that I suck at all the things that the obligatory wedding reading asked of me, I will try to round this out to make myself look at least somewhat desirable so you remember why you married me.

1. I cook for you. This is not a trivial thing since you've learned that I actually hate cooking, just despise it. I'm a good cook. I can make anything taste fantastic, even cauliflower and Brussel sprouts. I will continue to serve up the baked and basted meats, fried potatoes, and endless amounts of gravy

with a side of the surprisingly good I-tricked-you-into-eating-healthy vegetables because I love you.

2. I'm fantastic to talk to about politics, religion, and cheese. Summarily, we agree on these topics so it's always entertaining to discuss our angst when we're on the same page. We're both skeptical of the opposite spectrums of James Carville and Mary Matlin's marriage, but they probably like the same other things, such as historical fiction vs. Louis LaMour or taking vacations to tour historical places, not tour other people's farms. Even when we have slightly differing opinions, we know that no matter what, we'll both have cheese (except I want no part of that one from Aldi that tasted like feet).
3. I can make light of our pretend-we-are-poor lifestyle (99% of the time). Yes, technically, I am poor. I have squandered my hard-earned savings on staying at home with two little monkeys, but I still assume you bury money in the yard that amounts to what Howard Hughes spent on Kleenex. Millions, it must be millions! I know if I can handle a car that looks like it's hanging on by duct tape and a prayer for as long as possible, I'll get an amazing vacation in return. If I can hang our clothes out to dry, even during the winter time (when there's a perfectly good dryer in the bathroom) then I will be well stocked on wine. And if I am willing to wash your cow poop riddled pants, then I'm allowed to steal the change from your pockets to send our children to fancy summer camps where they learn to become kindergarten engineers or sea monster hunters. Marriage is give-and-take, borrow or steal, or just survive the ups and downs until your kids grow up and you like each other again.

All kidding aside, the reading from Corinthians boils down to finding someone who accepts your faults and has the same compass as you do. We have the same compass. We both have dreams that we haven't given up on. We both have beliefs that we live every day. We both want the world to be a better place for our children and we strive to make it just that. Thank you for putting up with me and fighting this battle.

Life Quote: She's my old lady! ~ What my husband yells at our children when they fight over me.

ACKNOWLEDGEMENTS

This book has been a dream. Not the actual editing or formatting, which were processes straight from hell, but a literal dream of mine for as long as I can remember. When I was young, I was editor, author, and cartoonist for the *NF Star*, a newspaper I created in my bedroom, hand-delivered to my neighbors' mailboxes (which turns out is illegal), and lasted for the better part of a summer. This was before home scanners and printers. I spent an endless amount of time painstakingly copying the handwritten pages, and now that I'm a parent, I realize my mom must have been ecstatic with all the quiet time she had while I obsessed over my new passion. I bet that's when she started drinking and reading, but that summer was over quickly and I'm pretty sure the same wine and books purchased that summer are still collecting dust in her house.

Quickly, I saw that newswriting was not my thing because none of my neighbors were paying their subscription bills, cheap bastards (it was only a quarter). I cannot be deterred so I swung full force into the second least profitable form of writing - creative writing. My poor grade school teachers had to deal with my endless stories, and when I declared my creative writing major, my college professors first asked, "What are you going to do with that?" and then stated, "I didn't even know that was an option for a major."

I've spent years putting it down and starting up again, writing many first chapters, first 100 pages, first 200 pages before putting them away as well. Then I started the *Desperate Farmwives* blog as a quick outlet for my writing and it narrowed my focus and gave me an outlet to combine my favorite things: writing, humor, and family.

No way, no how, could I have done this on my own. I have many to thank for encouraging or inspiring my madness.

First, to the sweet teacher who couldn't get rid of me after high school and was kind enough to edit my book. I'm an adult so I will use your full name even though I always forget in person and call you Ms. Hoefer out of habit: Sharon Hoefer. You had to deal with my run-on sentences, explosion of commas, and complete hyperbole in high school and now currently. It's great to know there's no shortage of red ink or awesome role models to go around. You were and always will be a great educator, and I can't thank you enough for not only editing this book, but teaching me so many life lessons, the most important of all, to not be a bystander in life.

Also, a tremendous thank you to Becky Huntsman, a retired English teacher, current public librarian, and all around great human being, who edited this book as well. You always have a smiling face, time to chat with the moms (me) who have been stuck at home all day, and you never chide me for my overdue books and MIA library card.

Since I mentioned the library, I must also thank the whole library staff for being there to cheer me on when I realized my Chromebook and MacBook weren't going to make the cut on some of the things I wanted to do. Back to a PC with Microsoft Word, which meant frequent trips to the library. You all were so nice to share some positivity and tell me to get back to work when you saw that I was procrastinating. Dear Readers, if you haven't frequented your public library lately, you should. They are amazing!

Speaking of squatting in other places, I also have to thank Rachel Brown of Rachel Brown Art for giving me an outlet for my need to tackle projects head first and for providing a quiet place so I could get my own projects done. I loved working around Sherry, Tina, and no one cheers you on like Humphrey.

I also have to thank the great women in my life for offering encouragement all the time, chocolate as the carrot to get me over the finish line, and wine, lots of wine, when I needed a distraction, or even when I didn't.

My mother has been a great help, watching my sons when I needed time to work, and she must be sorely disappointed because she was really hoping that "work" meant I was spending time with my husband making another baby. The women at the Boonslick Women's Business Network gave me endless motivation. To see 30 or more women over the last two years also juggling 20 different jobs and having the energy to still mentor others kept me going. Also, I have been motivated by my other group of mentors from the group Badass Women Writers Getting Shit Done (yeah, that's their name, straight up gangster!). These ladies are generous, insightful, inspirational, and yeah, badasses. You're a group of poetry, sci-fi, fantasy, nonfiction, and fiction writers and you welcomed me and my idea of writing a funny little book about my life and thought it was a great idea. Thank you so much!

I also have to thank the other desperate farmwives in my life. I have to thank my mother-in-law for the stories I have stolen and for watching my monster boys and filling them full of homemade, preservative free muffins when I would have handed them a Pop-Tart. She jumped right into a dairy farm life when she was newly married and still embraces farm life today. She may even enjoy it more than my father-in-law. Without your perseverance, there wouldn't be a farm to come home to. My sister-in-law is the wise woman who came up with the desperate farmwives blog idea, or maybe I did. We were drinking wine and I really don't remember. She has encouraged my stories, I have included some of hers, and she's always had wine and bean dip at our "business meetings." I must also thank the original desperate farm wife, Grandma Willie. You never pulled any punches when talking about how hard marriage is, you nagged your husband like it was going out of style, and you were the one who laid the smackdown on my husband when he suggested cloth diapers. I can't express my gratitude in words. We miss you dearly. I want to be Grandma Willie when I grow up.

I have to thank my children for giving me a new outlook on life. It's okay to look goofy; it's actually a must. Who cares what others think as long as you're happy. Just like a little boy who finds happiness discovering whatever dirt he can roll around in, I found the core of what makes me happy, even if it means I might look a little silly. People really love it when I look silly. I must give the audience what it wants. My boys are also slowly teaching me that laughter is contagious, a bath is optional, and if you're going to toot near Daddy, you better run.

Speaking of my husband, last but not least, I must thank him. He has a good sense of humor, obviously. I think he enjoys being picked on. He's not embarrassed by any of the cheap tricks he has. He loves to tell people how much his Festiva cost him and how many miles per gallon he gets. He loves to show people *Farm Show* reusables around our farm. He loves being the envy of the county during a drought when he has round bales piled up all over the place from someone begging to get rid of it the previous year. It may be old, but it's cheaper than grain. Even though I secretly think he loves my stories, I must thank him for allowing me to share them and for giving me time to share them. I must also apologize to him because while he took the boys out of the house so I could write, I spent half the time working on a 1000-piece puzzle, folding laundry while I watched *The Tudors,* and stealing change from his pockets while sorting laundry. A writer needs to find focus and I find it when I know I have a quarter for an Aldi shopping cart. I love you, my world-traveling, anti-social, adventure-seeking, afraid-of-heights husband. You're the King Louie to my Marie Antoinette….sorry, I led you into this mess.

ABOUT THE AUTHOR

Elisha Wells Stroupe is the creator and author of the blog *Desperate Farmwives* and owner and designer of HoCo Media, a digital and print advertising and publishing company. She lives in mid-Missouri with her two boys and her husband, but she is planning a life of world travel as soon as she can convince her husband that traveling and socializing with others is not as dangerous and unpleasant as he makes it out to be.

Made in the USA
Lexington, KY
06 December 2019

58251727R00125